STUDIES IN AFRICAN LITERATURE

African Writers
on African Writing

▼▼▼▼▼▼▼▼▼▼▼▼▼▼▼▼▼▼▼▼▼▼▼▼▼▼▼▼▼▼▼▼

KILLAM, G. D., ed. African writers on African writing. Northwestern, 1973. 172p (Studies in African literature) 72-97110. 5.00, 2.50 pa. ISBN 0-8101-0411-3
A collection of 16 previously published essays by 14 of Africa's best-known creative writers, which brings together materials scattered in many periodicals which are accessible only in larger university libraries. Short biographical notes are provided on each writer. The original sources are listed on the acknowledgements page. They include essays, speeches, and interviews, and so vary in depth of coverage and style. Novels, poetry, and drama are discussed in reference to teaching, nationalism, literary criticism, language forms, and realistic sociocultural content. The coverage differs from *African writers talking,* edited by Pieterse and Duerden (CHOICE, June, 1973). Useful for graduate and undergraduate collections which include the works of contemporary African creative writers. Index of authors and titles.

African Writers
on African Writing

EDITED BY G. D. KILLAM

NORTHWESTERN UNIVERSITY PRESS

EVANSTON

1973

G. D. Killam is Professor of English at York University, Toronto,
and Visiting Professor of English at the University of Dar es Salaam.

This book is Dedicated
to the Memory of
Frank Bessai

Contents

Acknowledgements

▼▼▼▼▼▼▼▼▼▼▼▼▼▼▼▼▼▼▼▼▼▼▼▼▼▼▼▼▼▼▼▼▼▼▼▼

The authors and editors of the following are thanked for permission to reproduce articles:

Black Academy Review. Vol. 1, No. 1 (Spring, 1970), S. Okechukwu Mezu 'Poetry and Revolution in Modern Africa'.

Black Orpheus. 19 (1966), pp. 48–54, Lewis Nkosi, 'Fiction by Black South Africans'. Vol. 2, No. 3, pp. 14–23 'The Patriot as Writer.'

Ibadan University Press. 'The Writers Speak' from *African Literature and the Universities*, 1965 (Papers presented at the First Festival of Negro Arts, Dakar).

Negro Digest. XV, 9 (July 1966), pp. 39–46 for Nkosi, Rubadiri and Kariuki, 'African Literature Today: Relating Literature and Life'.

New African. 52, 1969. Ama Ata Aidoo, 'No Saviours'.

New Statesman. January 29, 1965, pp. 161–162 Chinua Achebe, 'The Novelist as Teacher'.

Nigeria Magazine. 75 (1962), pp. 61–62 Chinua Achebe, 'Where Angels Fear to Tread'; 81 (1964), pp. 157–160 Chinua Achebe, 'The Role of the Writer in a New Nation'; 89 (1966), pp. 118–126 J. P. Clark, 'Aspects of Nigerian Drama'.

Présence Africaine. English Edition XXX, 58 (1966), Cheikh Hamidou Kane, 'The African Writer and his Public'.

Transition. III, 10 (1963), pp. 15–16 Gabriel Okara, 'African Speech . . . English Words'; IV, 15 (1964), pp. 39–42 David Rubadiri, 'Why African Literature'.

Times Literary Supplement. August 11, 1961, pp. 520–523, Nadine Gordimer, 'The Novel and the Nation in South Africa'.

Ba Shiru. Autumn 1970–Spring 1971, University of Wisconsin, 'Interview with Okello Oculi'.

Northwestern University Press. Ali A. Mazrui, 'The Patriot as an Artist'. Material for this essay is drawn from Ali A. Mazrui's longer work, *Cultural Engineering and National Building in East Africa* (Northwestern University Press, Evanston, 1972).

Introduction

▼▼

THE writers whose essays and articles are reproduced here speak for themselves on a variety of related literary and social issues, so there is no need for an elaborate introduction. The essays range in time over the last ten years and over the face of Africa. Most of the writers included are now known, not only throughout Africa, but in many other places of the world. While an attempt has been made to provide a balanced collection representing East, West and South Africa, nevertheless there have been some problems over copyright, as, for instance, with the publishers of Ezekiel Mphahlele. It was also felt that, as Ngugi had collected his essays under the title of *Homecoming* and as they would be published at about the same time as this book, it was unnecessary to make them available here merely for the sake of being representative.

Modern African writing in English has established its presence and reputation quickly in the last twenty years. It seems a good time to bring together articles by African writers where they discuss their craft, their art and their purposes as writers. However, in an article 'Poetry in Africa Today', published elsewhere, J. P. Clark reminds us of the 'pioneer' and 'pilot' poets of West Africa, Michael Dei-Anang of Ghana and Chief Dennis Osadebay of Nigeria and makes miscellaneous reference to African writers of the late nineties and early twentieth century.

Modern African writing has now achieved significant audiences in Africa and is gaining an audience throughout the world. Bibliographies of the imaginative writing produced by Africans in any given year now run to many pages; there are journals devoted to considering African writing, and conferences and seminars held frequently (both inside and outside Africa) to discuss it. The essays included here, chosen from various sources, are arranged in alphabetical order by author. It might be possible to arrange these pieces under such subject headings as 'political comment', 'literary comment', 'comment on colonialism'; or simply under such headings as 'the novel', 'poetry' and 'drama'. But such ordering is arbitrary and not particularly helpful, since the remarks one writer may have to make about, for example, poetry, its production and function, will be relevant to the writing of fiction or drama, in both aesthetic and general social terms, as well as to the work and comment of other writers.

African literature is, like all literature, an end in itself: it reveals a human need to create, to make discoveries about the greater potentialities of self which satisfy man. Like all literatures, then, it needs no special justification. Nevertheless, most African writers have felt from the beginning, and especially since the early 1950s, a special obligation to the societies in which they function; they have determined that literature has a social function to interpret and educate society. This commitment – or rather the intensity of this commitment – probably arises out of the recognition that the colonial experience in Africa was particularly intense, however brief. African writers, unlike writers in some other countries with similar colonial pasts, have not turned their backs on their own cultures but have faced up to the many problems – political, social, educational, and cultural – which colonialism produced and have sought solutions for them in imaginative form. That is, African literature speaks primarily for and to the people of its own country, and expresses their hopes and fears and aspirations. Moreover, it reasserts the uniqueness and dignity of their communities, things they were perilously close to losing as a result of colonialism. At the same time African writing seeks to identify those things of real value to contemporary African society in the colonial experience.

Specifically, the essays offered here reveal three essential and related concerns: Firstly, with the social-political function of literature. Secondly, they debate and seek to establish the place of African literature within the traditions of English literature; all of these writers have some comment to make, either directly or implicitly, on this question. Thirdly, what these commentaries reveal is the uniquely African quality of African literature and of the African society which the literature reflects; this, in the end, accounts for its success. In their various ways, these essays reveal that African writers are prepared to submit their work to a scrutiny which has the rigour of systematic literary study, an exercise especially important at a time when, as Achebe points out, 'some publishers will issue any trash that comes out of Africa because Africa has become the fashion. In this situation there is real danger that some writers may not be patient enough and disciplined enough to pursue excellence in their work'. This is to say that there is a concern with standards of writing, since the writer's ultimate activity is 'aesthetic' and his 'art' matters to him.

There is, as well, an urgent concern with standards beyond those of art. At present there is rapid change going on everywhere in Africa, and these essays reveal the writers' recognition that they have a special role to play in suggesting the basic values of a society; in reconciling the individual with his past and with his present culture in a time of crisis; in creating understanding and a sense of balance, in promoting tolerance. None of these tasks is easy in the face of the quest for power, position, wealth, economic development, and political sovereignty. The role of the writer is, in part, to find in the aspirations of his society new ways of seeking understanding in the light of traditional values as they are confronted with the impact of modern ideas. Ultimately, this is what the essays are about. They illuminate the novels and poetry and plays of the people who produced them.

Chinua Achebe

▼▼▼▼▼▼▼▼▼▼▼▼▼▼▼▼▼▼▼▼▼▼▼▼▼▼▼

The Novelist as Teacher

[1965]

WRITING of the kind I do is relatively new in my part of the world and it is too soon to try and describe in detail the complex of relationships between us and our readers. However, I think I can safely deal with one aspect of these relationships which is rarely mentioned. Because of our largely European education our writers may be pardoned if they begin by thinking that the relationship between European writers and their audience will automatically reproduce itself in Africa. We have learnt from Europe that a writer or an artist lives on the fringe of society – wearing a beard and a peculiar dress and generally behaving in a strange, unpredictable way. He is in revolt against society, which in turn looks on him with suspicion if not hostility. The last thing society would dream of doing is to put him in charge of anything.

All that is well-known, which is why some of us seem too eager for our society to treat us with the same hostility or even behave as though it already does. But I am not interested now in what writers expect of society; that is generally contained in their books, or should be. What is not so well documented is what society expects of its writers.

I am assuming, of course, that our writer and his society live in the same place. I realize that a lot has been made of the allegation that African writers have to write for European and American readers because African readers where they exist at all are only interested in reading textbooks. I don't know if African writers always have a foreign audience in mind. What I do know is that they don't have to. At least I know that I don't have to. Last year the pattern of sales of *Things Fall Apart* in the cheap paperback edition was as follows: about 800 copies in Britain; 20,000 in Nigeria; and about 2,500 in all other places. The same pattern was true also of *No Longer at Ease*.

Most of my readers are young. They are either in school or college or have only recently left. And many of them look to me as a kind of teacher. Only the other day I received this letter from Northern Nigeria:

Dear C. Achebe,

I do not usually write to authors, no matter how interesting their work is, but I feel I must tell you how much I enjoyed your editions of *Things Fall Apart* and *No Longer at Ease*. I look forward to reading your new edition *Arrow of God*. Your novels serve as advice to us young. I trust that you will continue to produce as many of this type of books. With friendly greetings and best wishes.

Yours sincerely,

I. Buba Yero Mafindi

It is quite clear what this particular reader expects of me. Nor is there much doubt about another reader in Ghana who wrote me a rather pathetic letter to say that I had neglected to include questions and answers at the end of *Things Fall Apart* and could I make these available to him to ensure his success at next year's school certificate examination. This is what I would call in Nigerian pidgin 'a how-for-do' reader and I hope there are not very many like him. But also in Ghana I met a young woman teacher who immediately took me to task for not making the hero of my *No Longer at Ease* marry the girl he is in love with. I made the kind of vague noises I usually make whenever a wise critic comes along to tell me I should have written a different book to the one I wrote. But my woman teacher was not going to be shaken off so easily. She was in deadly earnest. Did I know, she said, that there were many women in the kind of situation I had described and that I could have served them well if I had shown that it was possible to find one man with enough guts to go against custom?

I don't agree, of course. But this young woman spoke with so much feeling that I couldn't help being a little uneasy at the accusation (for it was indeed a serious accusation) that I had squandered a rare opportunity for education on a whimsical and frivolous exercise. It is important to say at this point that no self-respecting writer will take dictation from his audience. He must remain free to disagree with his society and go into rebellion against it if need be. But I am for choosing my cause very carefully. Why should I start waging war as a Nigerian newspaper editor was doing the other day on the 'soul-less efficiency' of Europe's industrial and technological civilization when the very thing my society needs may well be a little technical efficiency?

My thinking on the peculiar needs of different societies was sharpened when not long ago I heard an English pop song which I think was entitled 'I Ain't Gonna Wash for a Week'. At first I wondered why it should occur to anyone to take such a vow when there were so many much more worthwhile resolutions to make. But later it dawned on me that this singer belonged to the same culture which in an earlier age of self-satisfaction had blasphemed and said that cleanliness was next to godliness. So I saw him in a new light – as a kind of divine administrator of vengeance. I make bold to say, however, that his particular offices would not be required in my society because we did not commit the sin of turning hygiene into a god.

Needless to say, we do have our own sins and blasphemies recorded against our name. If I were God I would regard as the very worst our acceptance – for whatever reason – of racial inferiority. It is too late in the day to get worked up about it or to blame others, much as they may deserve such blame and condemnation. What we need to do is to look back and try and find out where we went wrong, where the rain began to beat us.

Let me give one or two examples of the result of the disaster brought upon the African psyche in the period of subjection to alien races. I remember the shock felt by Christians of my father's generation in my village in the early forties when for the first time the local girls' school performed Nigerian dances at the anniversary of the coming of the gospel. Hitherto they had always put on something Christian and civilized which I believe was called the Maypole dance. In those days – when I was grow-ing up – I also remember that it was only the poor benighted heathen who had any use for our local handicraft, e.g. our pottery. Christians and the well-to-do (and they were usually the same people) displayed their tins and other metal-ware. We never carried water pots to the stream. I had a small cylindrical biscuit-tin suitable to my years while the older members of our household carried four-gallon kerosene tins.

Today things have changed a lot, but it would be foolish to pretend that we have fully recovered from the traumatic effects of our first confrontation with Europe. Three or four weeks ago my wife, who teaches English in a boys' school, asked a pupil why he wrote about winter when he meant the harmattan. He said the other boys would call him a bushman if he did such a thing! Now, you wouldn't have thought, would you, that there was some-thing shameful in your weather? But apparently we do. How can this great blasphemy be purged? I think it is part of my business as a writer to teach that boy that there is nothing disgraceful about the African weather, that the palm-tree is a fit subject for poetry.

Here then is an adequate revolution for me to espouse – to help my society regain belief in itself and put away the complexes of the years of denigration and self-abasement. And it is essentially a question of education, in the best sense of that word. Here, I think, my aims and the deepest aspirations of my society meet. For no thinking African can escape the pain of the wound in our soul. You have all heard of the African Personality; of African democracy, of the African way to socialism, of negritude, and so on. They are all props we have fashioned at different times to help us get on our feet again. Once we are up we shan't need any of them any more. But for the moment it is in the nature of things that we may need to counter racism with what Jean-Paul Sartre has called an anti-racist racism, to announce not just that we are as good as the next man but that we are much better.

The writer cannot expect to be excused from the task of re-education and regeneration that must be done. In fact he should march right in front. For he is after all – as Ezekiel Mphahlele says in his *African Image* – the sensitive point of his community. The Ghanaian professor of philosophy, William Abraham, puts it this way:

> Just as African scientists undertake to solve some of the scientific problems of Africa, African historians go into the history of Africa, African political scientists concern themselves with the politics of Africa; why should African literary creators be exempted from the services that they themselves recognize as genuine?

I for one would not wish to be excused. I would be quite satisfied if my novels (especially the ones I set in the past) did no more than teach my readers that their past – with all its imperfections – was not one long night of savagery from which the first Europeans acting on God's behalf delivered them. Perhaps what I write is applied art as distinct from pure. But who cares? Art is important but so is education of the kind I have in mind. And I don't see that the two need be mutually exclusive. In a recent anthology A Hausa folk-tale, having recounted the usual fabulous incidents, ends with these words:

> They all came and they lived happily together. He had several sons and daughters who grew up and helped in raising the standard of education of the country.

As I said elsewhere, if you consider this ending a naïve anti-climax then you cannot know very much about Africa.

▼▼▼▼▼▼▼▼▼▼▼▼▼▼▼▼▼▼▼▼▼▼▼▼▼▼▼▼▼▼

Where Angels Fear to Tread

[1962]

MOST Nigerian writers have at one time or another complained about European (and American) critics. The most recent example was the article by J. P. Clark in the last number of *Nigeria Magazine* entitled 'Our Literary Critics'. Does all this mean that

Nigerian writers are intolerant of criticism as one of the assaulted critics has suggested?

I don't think so. Anyone who knows the Nigerian literary scene must be aware of the constant swiping that goes on all around. Some observers at the last Writers' Conference in Uganda commented on the way we criticized ourselves and poked fun at each other's work without rancour. No. We are not opposed to criticism but we are getting a little weary of all the special types of criticism which have been designed for us by people whose knowledge of us is very limited. Perhaps being unused to the in-fighting which is part of the racket of European and American literary criticism, we tend to be unduly touched and sometimes use extravagantly strong language in reply. I have been a little concerned at the involuntary shrillness which has lately crept into my own voice. Only the other day I wrote in an unworthy access of anger that Europeans can never understand us and that they ought to shut their traps. I now want to look at the matter again as coldly as possible and try to reach a few tentative conclusions.

The first big point to remember is that Nigerian writers cannot eat their cake (or *eba*, or whatever they eat) and have it. They cannot borrow a world language to write in, seek publication in Europe and America and then expect the world not to say something about their product, even if that were desirable. No, we have brought home ant-ridden faggots and must be ready for the visit of lizards. In part we should see it as a great compliment that in the ten years since we first broke into the world with *Palm-Wine Drinkard* we are already engaging seriously the attention of critics.

The question then is not whether we should be criticized or not but what kind of criticism. We as writers cannot of course, choose the kind of criticism we shall get. But surely we can say why we hate a lot of what we get.

I can distinguish three broad types of critics. First, the peevishly hostile, what-do-they-think-they-are, Honor Tracey breed. These are angry with the new-fangled ideas of colonial freedom and its gross ingratitude for colonial benefits, and they take it out on our literature. They won't be missed.

Then there are others who are amazed that we should be able to write at all, and in their own language too! I must admit they have their heart in the right place – rather like the German traveller who published a book, *Through African Doors*, recently. This man made a number of discoveries, one of which was that African food was not really monotonous as some people thought although, it must be admitted that its colour rarely deviates from red, green and yellow. Was it any wonder, he asked, that the flags of Ghana, Guinea and Cameroun were red, green and yellow!

This type (whether he is a critic or a writer) won't be missed very much.

Fortunately there is a third group which is fully conscious of the folly of the other two, and is bent on restoring a sense of balance to the argument. This third group says: We must apply to these African writers the same stringent standards of literary criticism with which we judge other writers. We don't have to pat them on the back and make them think they have already written masterpieces when we know they haven't.

This is a group with whom we could hold a dialogue, with frankness on either side. So let us begin.

This group annoys us by their increasing dogmatism. The other day one of them spoke of the great African novel yet to be written. He said the trouble with what we have written so far, is that it has concentrated too much on society and not sufficiently on individual characters and as a result it has lacked 'true' aesthetic proportions. I wondered when this *truth* became so self-evident and who decided that (unlike the other self-evident truth) this one should apply to black as well as white.

It is all this cock-sureness which I find so very annoying.

Another European critic was writing recently about Cyprian Ekwensi's *Burning Grass*. It was clear that this critic preferred it to the author's earlier books, *People of the City* and *Jagua Nana*. So far so good. But the critic went further to make pronouncements she was not qualified to make. She said of *Burning Grass*: 'This is truly Nigeria and these are *real* Nigerian people.' She did not say what her test was for sorting out real Nigerians from unreal ones and what makes say, Jagua less real than Sunsaye. And as if that was not enough, this critic went on to say that Ekwensi was much more at home in a rural setting than in big cities!

This kind of judgement is made all too frequently by Europeans who think they have special knowledge of Africa.

Let us examine for a brief moment the quality of this special knowledge.

I had a European friend Mr X, who was very fond of his steward whom we shall call Cletus. Mr X found Cletus terribly amusing because his inadequate knowledge of English made him say things in a fresh and funny way just as a child does when it is learning to talk. Mr X spoke of Cletus' infantile qualities with affectionate indulgence. 'He is a rogue', said Mr X, 'but a nice sort of rogue.'

I used to speak to Cletus in Ibo and I knew that he was a shrewd go-getter, neither shallow nor very amusing.

If Mr X had been a novelist he might have written about Cletus the harmless, 'I-like-Master-too-much' steward, and other Europeans would have said 'How true! Real Nigeria!'

I am not saying that the picture of Nigeria and Nigerians painted by a conscientious European must be invalid. I think it could be terribly valid, just as a picture of the visible tenth of an iceberg is valid.

I am sure that European writers on Africa are conscious of this kind of validity hence their efforts to describe the other nine tenths. The result is the man-of-two-worlds bogey – something lurking down there beyond the reach of Western education, the Guinea 'Stamp of one defect'.

But theories and bogeys are no substitute for insight. No man can understand another whose language he does not speak (and 'language' here does not mean simply words, but a man's entire world view). How many Europeans and Americans have our language? I do not know of any, certainly not among our writers and critics.

This naturally applies also in reverse, although our position is somewhat stronger because we have a good deal of European history, philosophy, culture, etc. in books. Even so, I would not dream of constructing theories to explain 'the European mind' with the same 'bold face' that some Europeans assume in explaining ours. But perhaps I am too diffident and ought to have a go at it. After all a novel is only a story and could be as tall as an iroko tree; in any case one couldn't do worse than the author of *Bribe Scorner* who invented an Ibo hero with a Yoruba name.

▼▼▼▼▼▼▼▼▼▼▼▼▼▼▼▼▼▼▼▼▼▼▼▼▼▼▼▼▼

The Role of the Writer in a New Nation

[1964]

ALTHOUGH I have cast the title of this lecture in rather general terms, I hope you will permit me to talk specifically of the role of the writer in a new *African* nation – and even more specifically still – the role of the writer in the new Nigeria.

It is natural for a people at the hour of their rebirth to cast around for an illustrious ancestor. The first Negro African state to win independence in recent times chose the name of the ancient kingdom of Ghana. Then Mali followed Ghana's example. Here in Nigeria, as you know, there was a suggestion to change the country's name to Songhai, the third of the great empires of the Sudan. Historians everywhere are re-writing the stories of the new nations – replacing short, garbled, despised history with a more sympathetic account. All this is natural and necessary. It is necessary because we must begin to correct the prejudices which generations of detractors created about the Negro. We are all familiar with the kind of thing I mean. If these prejudices were expressed only by the unenlightened it might be said that with the spread of enlightenment they would disappear. But men of distinction have been known to lend support to them.

Thomas Jefferson, the great theoretician of American freedom believed – at least in his active years – that Negroes have a lower grade of talent than whites.

The poet Kipling said something about black men being half-devil and half-child.

The famous humanitarian Albert Schweitzer sees no reason to doubt that he is the black man's brother; only he thinks of himself as the elder or the 'senior' brother.

One independent country in the African continent today is committed to the belief that the rule of white people is synonymous with civilization and the rule of black people is the negation of Christianity and civilization.

In a world bedevilled by these and much worse beliefs is it any wonder that black nations should attempt to demonstrate (sometimes with exaggerated aggressiveness) that they are as good as – and better than – their detractors?

This presents the African writer with a great challenge. It is inconceivable to me that a serious writer could stand aside from this debate or be indifferent to this argument which calls his full humanity in question. For me, at any rate there is a clear duty to make a statement. This is my answer to those who say that a writer should be writing about contemporary issues – about politics in 1964, about city life, about the last *coup d'etat*. Of course, these are all legitimate themes for the writer but as far as I am concerned the fundamental theme must first be disposed of. This theme – put quite simply – is that African people did not hear of culture for the first time from Europeans; that their societies were not mindless but frequently had a philosophy of great depth and value and beauty, that they had poetry and, above all, they had dignity. It is this dignity that many African people all but lost during the colonial period and it is this that they must now regain. The worst thing that can happen to any people is the loss of their dignity and self-respect. The writer's duty is to help them regain it by showing them in human terms what happened to them, what they lost. There is a saying in Ibo that a man who can't tell where the rain began to beat him cannot know where he dried his body. The writer can tell the people where the rain began to beat them. After all the writer's duty is not to beat this morning's headline in topicality, it is to explore in depth the human condition. In Africa he cannot perform this task unless he has a proper sense of history.

Let me give one small example to illustrate what I mean by people losing faith in themselves. When I was a schoolboy it was unheard of to stage Nigerian dances at any of our celebrations. We were told and we believed that our dances were heathen. The Christian and proper thing to do was for the boys to drill with wooden swords and the girls to perform, of all things, Maypole dances. Beautiful clay bowls and pots were only seen in the homes of the heathen. We civilized Christians used cheap enamel-ware from Europe and Japan; instead of water pots we carried kerosene cans. In fact, to say that a product was Ibo-made was to brand it with the utmost inferiority. When a people have reached this point in their loss of faith in themselves their detractors need do no more; they have made their point.

A writer who feels the need to right this wrong cannot escape the conclusion that the past needs to be recreated not only for the enlightenment of our detractors but even more for our own education. Because, as I said, the past with all its imperfections, never lacked dignity.

The question is how does a writer re-create this past? Quite clearly there is a strong temptation to idealize it – to extol its good points and pretend that the bad never existed.

When I think of this I always think of light and glass. When white light hits glass one of two things can happen. Either you have an image which is faithful if somewhat unexciting or you have a glorious spectrum which though beautiful is really a distortion. Light from the past passes through a kind of glass to reach us. We can either look for the accurate though somewhat unexciting image or we can look for the glorious technicolour.

This is where the writer's integrity comes in. Will he be strong enough to overcome the temptation to select only those facts which flatter him? If he succumbs he will have branded himself as an untrustworthy witness. But it is not only his personal integrity as an artist which is involved. The credibility of the world he is attempting to re-create will be called to question and he will defeat his own purpose if he is suspected of glossing over inconvenient facts. We cannot pretend that our past was one long, technicolour idyll. We have to admit that like other people's pasts ours had its good as well as its bad sides.

This is why, in spite of my great admiration for Camara Laye as a writer I must still say that I find *The Dark Child* a little too sweet. I admit that recollections of one's childhood tend naturally to be spread over with an aura of innocence and beauty; and I realize that Camara Laye wrote his book when he was feeling particularly lonely and home-sick in France. But I maintain that any serious African writer who wants to plead the cause of the past must not only be God's advocate, he must also do duty for the devil.

This is one of the things Wole Soyinka was saying in *A Dance of the Forests.* Those who want to resurrect an illustrious ancestor to grace their celebration may sometimes receive a great shock when the illustrious ancestor actually shows up. But, I think, it is still necessary that he should appear.

What I have said must not be understood to mean that I do not accept the present-day as a proper subject for the novelist. Far from it. My last but one novel is about the present day and the next one will again come up to date. But what I do mean is that owing to the peculiar nature of our situation it would be futile to try and take off before we have repaired our foundations. We must first set the scene which is authentically African; then what follows will be meaningful and deep. This, I think, is what Aimé Césaire meant when he said that the short cut to the future is via the past.

I realize that some writers particularly from South Africa may object strongly to what I have said. They may say 'we are not tribal any more; we live in cities; we are sophisticated. Why should we beat the drums of the old gods? This is precisely what Verwoerd wants us to do and we have no intention to oblige him.'

Perhaps they are right to feel this way; I just don't know. It is for them to discover how best to explore the human condition in their part of the continent. I speak for myself and this place and now. Sophistication is no substitute for a spiritual search for one's roots.

It is clear from what I have said so far that I believe the writer should be concerned with the question of human values. One of the most distressing ills which afflict new nations is a confusion of values. We sometimes make the mistake of talking about values as though they were fixed and eternal – the monopoly of Western civilization and the so-called higher religions. Of course, values are relative and in a constant state of flux.

Even within the Western civilization itself there is no unanimity, even within one country there are disagreements. Take the United States which is the most powerful country in the so-called Free World and whose constitution has inspired many a movement for equality and freedom. Does freedom there mean the same thing for everyone? For the late J. F. Kennedy and for the school children who shouted 'we are free' when they heard of his assassination or their elders who celebrated with champagne? Now if there can be so much confusion in an almost homogeneous culture how much more in an African country trying to build a modern state with tools fashioned in the tribe or clan? Some years ago – in 1958 or 59 – there was an accident at a dance in a Nigerian city. Part of the wall collapsed and injured many people – some seriously. Incredible as it may sound some car-owners at the dance refused to use their cars to convey the injured to hospital. One man was reported as saying that his seatcovers would be ruined.

The African writer may ask himself: Why was such callousness possible?
Is this an example of what some people have called the elemental cruelty of
the Negro? I am afraid it's nothing so fanciful. It merely shows a man who
has lost one set of values and has not yet acquired a new one – or rather has
acquired a perverted set of values in which seatcovers come before a
suffering human being. I make bold to say that such an incident could not
have happened in a well-knit traditional African society. But then you were
not obliged in those days to live next door to an enemy – as you have to do
today. In fact the whole concept of enemy and stranger has changed. So
we need a new set of values – a new frame of reference, a new definition of
stranger and enemy. The writer can help by exposing and dramatizing the
problem. But he can only do this successfully if he can go to the root of
the problem. Any incompetent newspaper man reports the incident of the
seatcovers. But you need a writer to bring out the human tragedy, the
crisis in the soul.

Take another example. Anyone who has given any thought to our society
must be concerned by the brazen materialism one sees all around. I have
heard people blame it on Europe. That is utter rubbish. In fact the
Nigerian society I know best – the Ibo society – has always been material-
istic. This may sound strange because Ibo life had at the same time a strong
spiritual dimension – controlled by gods, ancestors, personal spirits or *chi*,
and magic. The success of the culture was the balance between the two,
the material and the spiritual. But let no one under-rate the material side.
A man's position in society was usually determined by his wealth. All the
four titles in my village were taken – not given – and each one had its
price. But in those days wealth meant the strength of your arm. No one
became rich by swindling the community or (sic) stealing government
money. In fact a man who was guilty of theft immediately lost all his titles.
Today we have kept the materialism and thrown away the spirituality
which should keep it in check. Some of the chieftancy titles and doctorate
degrees we assume today would greatly shock our ancestors!

Let us mention just one more example of the crisis in our culture. Why
is it that Nigerians are content with shoddy work? Put a man to sweep this
room and in nine cases out of ten he will scamp through it leaving most of
it unswept. Why? Because it is government work, and government is alien,
a foreign body. When I was a boy, strangers from another part of Iboland
were coming for the first time to our village during the planting season to
work for the villagers for so much money and three meals a day. One day
one of these strangers came to plant my mother's coco-yams. At the end of
the day he received his pay, ate his last meal, and left. About two or three
weeks later the coco-yams began to sprout and the whole village saw what
this man had done.

When he had got tired of planting he had simply dug a big hole in the ground and buried a whole basket of coco-yams there. Of course by the time his crime was discovered he had left the village and was not likely to come back. Now this sort of crime is only possible when societies that were once strangers to one another suddenly began to mix. Apply this on a national sphere and you will begin to understand our problems. The village code of conduct has been violated but a more embracing and a bigger one has not been found.

The writer in our society should be able to think of these things and bring them out in a form that is dramatic and memorable. Above all, he has a responsibility to avoid shoddiness in his own work. This is very important today when some publishers will issue any trash that comes out of Africa because Africa has become the fashion. In this situation there is a real danger that some writers may not be patient enough and disciplined enough to pursue excellence in their work.

That brings me to the linguistic question. In this discussion I am leaving out writers in the various Nigerian languages. It is not that I under-rate their importance, but since I am considering the role of the writer in building a new nation I wish to concentrate on those who write for the *whole* nation whose audience cuts across tribe or clan. And these, for good or ill, are the writers in English.

For an African, writing in English is not without its serious set-backs. He often finds himself describing situations or modes of thought which have no direct equivalent in the English way of life. Caught in that situation he can do one of two things. He can try and contain what he wants to say within the limits of conventional English or he can try to push back those limits to accommodate his ideas. The first method produced competent, uninspired and rather flat work. The second method can produce something new and valuable to the English language as well as to the material he is trying to put over. *But* it can also get out of hand. It can lead to *bad* English being accepted and defended as African or Nigerian. I submit that those who can do the work of extending the frontiers of English so as to accommodate African thought-patterns must do it through their mastery of English and not out of innocence. Of course there is the obvious exception of Amos Tutuola. But even there it is possible that he has said something unique and interesting in a way that is not susceptible to further development. I think Gerald Moore in his *Seven African Writers* is probably right when he says of Tutuola that he stands at the end of a fascinating cul-de-sac. For the rest of us it is important first to learn the rules of English and afterwards break them if we wish. The good writers will know how to do this and the bad ones will be bad, anyway.

In closing let me remind you of a theme that has been recurring in Sedar

Senghor's thinking of late. He says that Africans must become producers of culture and not just its consumers.

African societies of the past, with all their imperfections, were not consumers but producers of culture. Anyone who reads Fagg's recent book *Nigerian Images* will be struck by the wealth and quality of the art which our ancestors produced in the past. Some of this work played a decisive role in the history of modern art. The time has come once more for us, artists and writers of today, to take up the good work and by doing it to enrich not only our own lives but the life of the world.

Ama Ata Aidoo

▼▼▼▼▼▼▼▼▼▼▼▼▼▼▼▼▼▼▼▼▼▼▼▼▼▼▼▼▼▼▼▼▼

No Saviours

[1969]

THE *Beautyful Ones Are Not Yet Born* by Ayi Kwei Armah has been published in the United States to what seems to be a torrent of controversy of the kind which seldom accompanies a first novel. But in spite of all the spate of words which is pouring out from professional reviewers about it, somehow it seems to me that the most interesting comment on it that has come to my notice so far, has been made by a friend and in a private letter: 'I have since read (the) novel . . . may be he wrote it to provoke, to irritate – but I think he overdid the tone of contempt . . . it is too aloof, in a foreign sort of way, like some report from a *casual foreign visitor who is visiting* a primitive society for the *first time* and is bent on *exposing* it in all its *primitivity, crudity* and so on. I can't take that from a fellow African.' (All emphasis mine, A A A.) I insist that this is the most important statement made so far on the *Beautyful Ones Are Not Yet Born* because its author (name withheld), without having any literary pretensions of his own, is nevertheless an extremely articulate African student, and by all regular standards, radical. Only the good Lord knows what is going to happen then when it is published for the British Publishers Traditional Market (!!) which solidly includes Ghana. Because if this young man who is not even from that country cannot take the novel, then one wonders how many of the English-reading Ghanaian 'elite' can.

The un-named hero is 'the man'. He is a worker on the railways. Born and bred in towns, he has no rural roots to escape to. He went to school but could not make the comfortable heights (University and equivalents) where once reached, one is protected from the harsh realities of *la vie Africaine*. The man represents the 'masses' whom all African politicians daily yap about but no one ever plans for. What distinguishes him from the ordinary worker though, is a mind and body which together form the nerve-centre of a radio-active kind of searchlight which probes all that is Ghana and of Ghanaians. What is revealed is not in fact the horrors of 'primitive Africa' but the nauseous essence of Africa civilized. For in so far as the 'modern' Ghanaian is not in any way different from any other 'modern African' (except perhaps by a higher degree of scepticism!) what the man knows about the country reads like a case-book on African corruption. It is of such incredible filth and shit and stink, it will make anybody puke. One automatically holds one's nose with disgust – literally too. Only the peasantry is spared. And perhaps this tells us something about the author's life. But more important: if we are aware of Frantz Fanon, we would realize how crucial this reluctance to discuss the peasantry is, in terms of the author's perception of what can operate revolutionarily in Africa. He wrote about the dead and not even the dying. 'When this caste has vanished, devoured by its own contradictions, it will be seen that nothing new has happened since independence was proclaimed, and that everything must be started again from scratch.'[1]

It is quite clear that the main thesis behind the story is that what we see around us of the so-called modern Africa is nothing but one messy offal. A mess in which everybody from the establishments to the most oppressed urban worker is caught, irredeemably. The leaders are busy swindling the people with meaningless verbiage. And the people, frustrated and bewildered, are cynically looking out for ways, very often shady, out of their nightmares. But then, the latter are just going round in circles since there are no ways out. It is a funny story; African funny: ' . . . There is no difference then. No difference at all between the white men and their apes, the lawyers and the merchants, and the apes of the apes, our Party men.' 'And it is also a Third World tale told with rare bitterness.' . . . So it should be easy now to see there have never been people to save anybody but themselves, never in the past, never now, and there will never be any saviours if each will not save himself. No saviours. Only the hungry and the fed.

Indeed, it could be quite misleading to approach the book as though it is just a novel in any 'traditional' sense of the word. It might be that as well but for all practical purposes, it is an intellectual exercise executed with rather formidable precision. There is nothing out of place. In fact, sometimes, one feels that there is too much in one place especially in the author's efforts always to make physical decay symbolize or correspond to spiritual degeneration. But then, it could also be proposed that he packed up the atmosphere precisely to show how stuffy it is. Everything has been thrown up and each has come up with a stench: from the Gold Coast of the years of political agitation against British colonial rule, ' . . . there were tales of white men with huge dogs that ate more meat in a single day than a human Gold Coast family got in a month, dogs which had as little love for black skins as their white masters,' through Nkrumah's Ghana, 'there was a lot of noise, for some time, about some investigation designed to rid the

[1] Frantz Fanon, *The Wretched of the Earth.*

country's trade of corruption. . . . The net had been made in the special Ghanaian way . . . to catch only the small dispensable fellows . . . And the big ones floated free, like all the slogans,' to post-coup Ghana, 'The policeman extracted money, rolling it up dexterously into an easy little ball hidden in his palm,' for nothing really had changed, only the set of people who would now be eating well!

There is something frightening about the book. And this is the clarity with which he has seen the African urban scene, as no visitor can be capable of, and the mercilessness with which he has opened it up – as no foreigner would dare do today. The following is only on a banister on a staircase of the 'Railway & Harbour Administration Block'. 'And the wood was not alone. Apart from the wood itself there were, of course, people themselves, just so many hands and fingers bringing help to the wood in its course towards putrefaction. Left-hand fingers in the careless journey from a hasty anus sliding all the way up the banister as their owners made the return trip from the lavatory downstairs to the offices above. Right-hand fingers still dripping with the after-piss and the stale sweat from fat crotches. The calloused palms of messengers after they had blown their clogged noses reaching for a convenient place to leave the well-rubbed moisture. Afternoon hands not entirely licked clean of palm soup and remnants of *Kenkey*. The wood would always win.' The condemnation is total. Of course it is too much and people would want to ask Armah what gives him the audacity to do this. For he does not even for a moment do us the kindness of letting us think that we are just the casualties of a colonial past. He makes it quite clear that we are dead. Not freshly dead. No, we've been dead a long time. Especially the politicians and pricking them with any sharp point releases such poisonous gas that only further poisons the terrible atmosphere symbolically, metaphorically and literally. The stink exists side by side and is part of the false 'gleam' of the post independence scene. Koomson 'the party man', surrounded by the beautiful and good things of life, his beautiful wife Estella of the soft hands, his smooth expensive car, his shining row of glasses. This socialist is inside, only a vessel carrying around so much rot. In the moments of extreme anxiety following the coup he is not only reduced to a whining animal, but the only other things which issue from him are farts. 'The smell was something the man had not at all expected. It was overpowering as if some corrosive gas, already half liquid, had filled the whole room, irritating not only the nostrils, but also the insides of eyes, ears, mouth and throat.'

The friend quoted earlier on is right of course. The author is contemptuous of us – but Lord, do we deserve it! The only consolation is that he, like the hero is of us too. For the hero, whom one might in haste almost think self-righteous in his seeming incorruptibility is after all, he whose mouth water had dropped on the bus seat at the beginning of the story and of course one wonders what elements in the insides of this good man could shoot off this disgusting liquid. Nor should we worry too much about what made Ayi Kwei Armah write this expose of his own people and in this almost masochistic manner. Perhaps it is pessimism, since at that level there is no involvement. And yet the fact of the novel itself is the proof of the author's concern. Perhaps it is just an honest description of how one man has seen his society. Certainly, he has spared himself and us either the pain of an Nkrumaist apologia or the terrible boredom of any anti-Nkrumaist pro-coup rubbish.

And his symbolism, both evocative and descriptive, is always dead accurate. The chichidoodoo bird, with its sad sweet song, wanting to eat worms but despising the filth that produces it is the hero, the society, and ironically the novel. Yet the *Beautyful Ones* is not an allegory. The characters he creates are too much alive. From the man to the unfortunate Maanan the prostitute who went mad with the colossal disappointment of what independence came to mean, each is there in his and her own right. The details are incredible. Poor Oyo, the man's wife, attempting to survive what to her is a degrading life by trying hard to impress involuntary listeners in public places with accounts of glories that were not, are not and never will be hers. Estella the beautiful, selfish and stupid wife of the party man, holding forth on socialism!!

Unfortunately, the only aspect of the book that is unclear concerns the role of the Teacher. One feels like asking the author for his true identity. Is he just a good man or does Ayi Kwei feel in spite of himself, that he ought to give us someone who is of us and yet wise enough to be our guiding light? And if so why does he envelop him in such mystery, this Plato–Aristotle quoting African philosopher?

Because of Ferdinand Oyono's *Houseboy*, one cannot say glibly that Armah's *Beautyful Ones Are Not Yet Born* is the 'deepest' modern African novel yet published. However, in what way the latter is different from the former shall be evident by and by. But we find here, the same awareness of the basic weakness Africans have exhibited over and over again since the beginning of our encounter with the West. That is, it seems not to matter what generation we belong to or what social class we come from, we have got this unhealthy attraction for 'the gleam'-ing and very often trashy products of someone else's civilization. And that this, more than anything else has been and is our undoing. Indeed, it is going to finish us completely unless a new generation is born which will be able to define the validities of life for itself (never mind what the white man or anyone says) and be prepared to take on fully, the responsibilities that will surely come with this definition. Furthermore for Armah at any rate, the present intellectuals and politicians are clearly irrelevant or worse: what little wisdom remains is with the people to whom he goes for imagery and symbolism and after all, the gorgeous title of the novel with its ungrammatical spelling of 'beautyfu'. He took it from the tailboard of a mammy wagon.

Meanwhile it should be remembered that this type of purgative exposure, however painful it is, is absolutely necessary, depending upon whether or not one believes that truth as represented in writing can be in any way effective in helping social change. If on the other hand, even those of us who basically agree with him on the need to have this kind of job done feel that he has killed a patient instead of performing a surgery (though knowing Ghanaians one wonders how such an accident can ever happen!) then we have a right to our anger. Especially when one considers the fact that certain sections of 'international opinion' which never rejoice at what is indicative of Africa's good have been praising the novel to God's own skies! One comforting thought though, is that at no point in the story does Ayi Kwei excuse the colonizers. Indeed, he seems to feel that one should spare as little of one's breath for them as possible. What he does proclaim aloud is that he thinks of us: those who are still having their civilized dialogues with the former oppressors of Africa and with them are busily consuming illegally the continent's strength and fertility. While at the same time – and this is the worst of all – they congratulate themselves on the excellent job they are doing, ushering Africa into the twentieth century. Perhaps, the beautiful ones, when they are born, and let's pray it will be soon, will take care of everything and everybody once and for all time. The least we can do is to wait.

J. P. Clark

▼▼▼▼▼▼▼▼▼▼▼▼▼▼▼▼▼▼▼▼▼▼▼▼▼▼▼▼▼▼▼

Aspects of Nigerian Drama[1]

[1966]

IF drama means the 'elegant imitation' of some action significant to a people, if this means the physical representation or the evocation of one poetic image or a complex of such images, if the vital elements to such representation or evocation are speech, music, ritual, song as well as dance and mime, and if as the Japanese say of their Noh theatre, the aim is to 'open the ear' of the mind of a spectator in a corporate audience and 'open his eyes' to the beauty of form, then there is drama in plenty in Nigeria, much of this as distinctive as any in China, Japan and Europe. But drama of what beginning? Of how many kinds? Of what form? In what language? And are its functions solely aesthetic and entertainment as in the West today or have these functions, in addition, ceremonial and spiritual relevance for both actors and spectators? To shed a measure of light upon a subject so much in the news these days and yet so much mis-understood by so many, there must be satisfactory answers found for these queries, and I dare say, several besides.

Of the origins of Nigerian drama very little is known that is reliable and precise, for the simple reason that no comprehensive study has been made so far of the subject either by the old government sociologists or by the new drama experts of today. But one fact is certain. Contrary to what some seem to think, Nigerian drama did not begin at the University of Ibadan. The roots go beyond there, and one hopes, they are more enduring than that. Very likely, they lie where they have been found among other peoples of the earth, deep in the past of the race. '... according to a widespread belief, which is not without a foundation in fact,' writes Sir James E. Frazer in *The Golden Bough*, 'plants reproduce their kinds through the

[1] *Aspects of Nigerian Drama* was first ad-libbed at the Teaching of English as a Second Language Workshop run by the Departments of Nigerian Languages and Linguistics and of Adult Education and Extramural Studies, University of Ibadan, 1964, and later read as a paper at the Seminar on Nigerian Literature organized by the English Association, University of Nigeria, Nsukka, 1966.

sexual union of male and female elements, and that on the principle of homoeopathic or imitative magic, this reproduction is supposed to be stimulated by the real or mock marriage of men and women who masquerade for the time being as spirits of vegetation. Such magical dramas have played a great part in the popular festivals of Europe, and based as they are on a very wide conception of natural law, it is clear that they must have been handed down from a remote antiquity.' We are told later this magical theory of the seasons became supplemented by a religious theory. 'For although men now attributed the annual cycle of change primarily to corresponding changes in their deities, they still thought that by performing certain magical rites they could aid the god, who was the principle of life, in his struggle with the opposing principle of death . . . *The ceremonies which they observed for this purpose were in substance a dramatic representation of the natural processes which they wished to facilitate* (italics are mine); for it is a familiar tenet of magic that you can produce any desired effect by merely imitating it. And as they now explained the fluctuations of growth and decay, of reproduction and dissolution, by the marriage, the death, and the rebirth or revival of the gods, the irreligious or rather magical dramas turned in great measure on these themes.' We have drawn extensively upon that well-worn handbook because we believe that as the roots of European drama go back to the Egyptian Osiris and the Greek Dionysius so are the origins of Nigerian drama likely to be found in the early religious and magical ceremonies and festivals of the peoples of this country. The *egungun* and *oro* of the Yoruba, the *egwugwu* and *mmo* masques of the Ibo, and the *owu* and *oru* water masquerades of the Ijaw are dramas typical of the national repertory still generally unacknowledged today.

Now Nigerian drama falls into two broad groups. One we may call traditional, the other modern drama. Of the first, still very much in the original state described by Frazer, we can again determine two main subgroups. One of these is sacred because its subjects and aims are religious, while the other is secular drama shading from the magical through a number of sub-kinds to the straight play and entertainment piece. Within the sacred species there are again two types: one grouping together what have been variously termed ancestral or myth plays, and the other which are masquerades or plays by age groups and cults. The dramas of *Obatala* and *Oshagiyan* performed annually at Oshogbo and Ejigbo provide indisputable examples of the first sacred kind. Against this set are the masquerades, for example, the *ekine* plays of Buguma.

Covering the Oshagiyan festival at Ejigbo, M. Pierre Verger, the French ethnologist shunting between Brazil and here, reports that a 'miniature war' opens the festival with a real bang. This is fought between the twin wards of Isale Osholo and Oke Mapo. 'Composed of attacks, hasty withdrawals and offensive sallies,' the battle is interspersed with periods of comparative calm, during which the combatants standing up their special fighting sticks 'no longer attack their enemies but shout invectives and insults at each other worthy of the age of Homer'. In earlier times, the fighting was simply symbolic, being staged between two priests. But the epic staging today calls up all able-bodied men of the clan so that they can taste of the injuries their ancestors administered on the Rainmaker who denied them rain. It is this version that M. Pierre Verger found still observed in Bahia today.

The annual ritual imprisonment of Obatala at Oshogbo is even more dramatic. The following is an account of the festival given by Chief Ulli Beier: 'The second day of the festival has a feature not unlike a passion play. There is no spoken dialogue but singing accompanies the perform- ance and the entire action is danced.

'The story is of a fight between the Ajagemo and another priest, bearing the title of Olunwi. Ajagemo is taken prisoner by Olunwi and carried off from the palace. The Oba, however, intervenes for his release. He pays ransome to Olunwi, and Ajagemo is liberated and allowed to return to the palace. The return gradually attains the qualities of a triumphal procession.

'The dancing of this simple (drama) as performed at Ede takes only a few minutes. But it is intensely moving largely because of the qualities put into his part by the Ajagemo. *There is no question of mere acting.* The ability to suffer and not to retaliate is one of the virtues every Obatala worshipper must strive to possess.'

These virtues of Obatala are not unlike those of the crucified Christ. Obatala in fact is the creation God of the Yoruba. Though all powerful he is gentle and full of love for all creation. In the legend, against the advice of the Oracle Ifa, Obatala, on his way to Sango, the God of thunder, relieves Eshu, the God of mischief, here disguised as an old woman, of a pot of oil. The pot breaks in the process with an effect like a sacred vessel breaking – which is not unlike that of opening Pandora's box! Thus Obatala, his white dress all dripping with oil, arrives at the court of King Sango at Oyo, and since nobody recognizes the God, he is thrown into jail when he protests at the ill-treatment of a horse. As a result, drought and famine befall the earth. And it is not until King Sango consults the oracle and is told he must make reparation to an innocent man wrongly punished in his Kingdom that the general curse is lifted. This is the story re-enacted in the annual ritual at Oshogbo and other Yoruba towns, a story which has informed my own problematic poem 'The Imprisonment of Obatala'.

In each case given above, the story derives directly from an ancestor or founder myth well-known to the audience, and the development is not so much by logic and discussion as by a poetic evocation of some religious experience shared alike by performer and spectators. For them the act is therefore one of worship and sacrifice.

A similar drama is described with tremendous power by Mr Chinua Achebe in *The Arrow of God*. This is *The First Coming of Ullu*, as celebrated in the market-place of 'the six villages of Umuaro' to the clamorous beat of the *ikolo* and *ogene*. The precipitate entrance of the protagonist priest Ezeulu, all got up in his regalia and waving his terrible Nne Ofo ahead of his assistants, the pantomime he breaks into, the monologue and incantation he says while the participating audience wave leaves of pumpkin in offerings of prayer, the dumping of these into a heap in burial of the sins of the land to the crescendo and crash of the *kome*, and the sudden stampede of the six settlements of Umuaro out of the square now inherited by spirits, this is highly stylized drama indeed. One can only hope that the great havoc and tornado that was Winterbota, I mean, Captain Winterbottom, Her Britannic Majesty's Political Agent accredited to one of the primitive tribes of the Lower Niger in their own interest and pacification, did not irrecoverably blow down this splendid institution of Ullu of the six settlements.

In all this the elements of pleasure and entertainment cannot be neatly pared from the devotion and ecstasy of religious worship. In the masquerade and age plays the aesthetic experience of the art undoubtedly is dominant. In fact the anthropologist Mr Robin Horton more or less states they are purely so. 'The ekine plays,' he writes of the New Year Festival of Buguma, 'are overtly religious in purpose, and those of the young men more or less unashamedly secular; both traditional and modern performances contain a very large element of sheer recreation. As art, all these masquerades are best judged as ballet rather than drama: though there is a plot of sorts running through many of them, it is at best very slight – rather a framework upon which to hang a dance sequence than something of value in itself. The leg of the dancer, not the story he enacts, is what Kalabari praise and criticize.' Mr Horton makes the same point in respect of the Amagba Festival at another Ijaw settlement, that of Kula, a point with which we are not wholly in agreement and hope to take up later.

It is in a similar vein the novelist-editor of *Nigeria Magazine*, Mr Onuora Nzekwu, reports on the production of the *Mingi Oporopo*, that is, the water-pig, at Opobo. 'The drama . . . reveals a high standard of play-acting . . . the various parts fit the daily life of the actors and tend to make the whole performance more real and natural. The play was enacted not in the river, but in the Amayanabo's compound. Of course, there was a canoe, paddles, a fishing net, representations of the shrines to the god of fortune.

Fish and the monster were represented by masquerades whose carved headpieces told the role each played. The headpiece, a large fish, depicting the monster and which can open and shut its mouth at will is a credit to the creative ability of these people.'

On the secular plane the stage is equally crowded. First, there are the 'magic' or trick plays and secondly the pastoral or puppet plays of Calabar described with such mixed feelings by that pro-consul and anthropologist P. A. Talbot. Incidentally, his works are quite a jungle – as thick as any he wandered through in Southern Nigeria at the beginning of the century. The interesting thing is that they carry in their labyrinthian way pathways that often lead to unexpected clearings and discoveries. One such surprise is his record of a number of plays performed for him during his tours among the Efik and Ibibio people. There was *The Tight-rope Dancer* or *The Second-Born Excels*; there was also *The Pole Play*.

He thought some of these mere 'conjuring tricks'; others he found to be 'gruesome plays', especially those in which either a baby was professedly pounded to death in a mortar and then brought to life again whole, or the decapitated head of a man was slapped back on his neck without apparent harm, or a man was impaled upon a spit without causing disgorgement of his bowels. Another was staged by ventriloquists. According to Talbot, this carried an incest interlude too 'vulgar' for entry into official files. 'I am happy to say', he makes the excuse, 'that this is the only occasion on which we have encountered an instance of real vulgarity among primitive African peoples. Up till now, even when turning on subjects usually avoided by Europeans on account of difficulty of treatment, the perfect simplicity of manner and purpose with which such were mentioned or explained robbed them of possible offence. In this one case, most unfortunately inexcusable and irrelevant coarseness showed itself, naked and unashamed, and we could not but wonder as to the influence to which the innovation was due.' What was this innovation that riled the old resident so? We gather it was open copulation between father and daughter-in-law. Obviously at that point of performance, life had overcome art.

But the day was not completely lost; in fact it had a splendid finale, one well worth the dangers of the expedition taken in a hammock. 'After the garishness and coarseness of the performance above described, we were quite unprepared for the beauty of that which was to follow.' This was the Akan play *Utughu* or *The Spider Play*. Preparations for it were always intense for 'as in everything African, Tragedy walked close upon the heels of Comedy'. Obviously very moved, Talbot goes on to describe the Female Figure in the special costume she wore at the point she does a death duet with her partner in this 'puppet' play. 'She wore a mask, brightest gold in colour, which, from the distance, looked as though it might have come straight from some Egyptian tomb. Here were the same long diamond-shaped eyes as those which gaze from old papyri or the walls of many a forgotten sepulchre, newly opened to the light of day, or such as are depicted on painted sarcophagi or the papyri of The Book of the Dead.' After the performance, Talbot's wish to have his wife photograph 'the loveliness of the gold-painted mask worn by the bird-wife' was granted by the Ibibio 'on the payment of the requested dash'. But then comes the shock. 'Our disillusionment may be imagined when the actual objects were laid in our hands. Carved from a solid block of wood, almost grotesque in outline, the whole glamour and beauty of the thing seemed to have disappeared by magic . . .' And this leads the man into glorious speculation. 'Thinking over the difference, scarce believable save to those who had actually witnessed it, a memory wave brought to mind visions of masks worn in the dramas of old Greece. There, too, the conditions were not unlike. Given as here, in the open – possibly also with a background of swaying palms – may not the glamour of air and sky have lent to these masks also, when seen from a distance, a beauty and aloofness which not only heightened the effect of the glorious text, but gave to the whole an atmosphere in which great men and women lived and acted greatly – far removed from the commonplaces of this workaday world?'

The point to remember in this gorgeous piece of rhetoric is that about the thin line existing between reality and illusion in the theatre. If as both Dr Johnson and Coleridge enjoin us, we never quite lose all our consciousness while willingly suspending our sense of disbelief, there will be no cause to rush the stage at the point Hamlet is hacking Laertes to death. This is a custom and convention strictly observed in many of our societies, else what prevents the housewife or child from telling the man from the mask? It will be good too to recognize a point about such comparisons. The implication is not that one group of people borrowed this and that property from another but that there can and in fact there do occur areas of coincidence and correspondence in the way of living among several peoples separated by vast distances and time, and who apparently are of distinct cultures, practices and persuasions. For example, the orchestra and the leader-chorus arrangement of characters occupies as much a principal part in Nigerian theatre as it did in Greek theatre. But this is not to say one is debtor to the other. It is a matter of correspondence and coincidence. Yeats observed this to be true, seeing in every Irish beauty a potential Helen full of havoc to the race. And the husband and wife team of Herskovits underline the fact with obvious excitement when in Dahomey they discovered in *The Lover and the Initiate*, a cult drama, the old Greek story of Alcestis. '(Here) the conventional unities are observed. The place is the cult-house; the action occurs during one day; the theme is love and the courage to defy the *Vodum* and Death in its name, until both are moved to pity.'

This leads us directly into our third class of secular drama – the civic kind. Mainly drawn from myths and rituals telling the history of the tribe, they serve a common civic purpose as do tales and fables, namely, that of educating and initiating the young into the secrets and moral code of society. It is interesting to note that both the period of eight years the Dahomean initiate was interned in the forest away from female contact and the purpose of turning him into a responsible citizen are themes that feature in the graduation drama of Isiji or Ipu Ogo performed by the Ibo people of Edda near Afikpo in the Eastern Provinces.

Another beautiful drama of the same class, associated with a figure of antiquity and now observed more or less as a vegetation festival is the annual *Igogo* at Owo in the West. The central figure is Orosen, wife of the founder of Owo. A changeling creature from the forest, the story of how her rival spouses eventually encompass her downfall by tricking their man into revealing the true identity of his favourite wife throws vivid light upon the conventional day-to-day conflicts and complexities obtaining in every house of polygamy.

Our fourth class of the secular kind consists of dance or song dramas such as the Udje of the Urhobo. The Udje, as we stated in an earlier paper published in this journal, 'is straight entertainment. That is, it is all art and little or no ritual and religion. . . . Performance is by age groups, wards and towns, each using the other as subject for its songs.' More often than not, the songs are straight satirical pieces, although a good number are parables passing oblique social comments and criticism. Supplemented with imitative action and movement, however much on a linear level, these song and dance-dramas never fail to reach their audience members of whom break out from time to time to mix in with the cast. Quite similar to these are the seasonal dance-dramas of the Ijaw, Ekpetese being easily the best-known of the lot. But that was thirty odd years ago, and besides, its stars and fans are all either faded or scattered.

Finally, the narrative or epic dramas which go on for days (seven is the magic number!) and which, because they demand so much energy and time, are more or less dying out today. A ready example is the Ijaw saga *Ozidi*. Out of this half drama, half narrative work I have just made a marathon play soon to be released by the Oxford University Press, while work is in progress now to publish the original story both in the Ijaw and English. It is the story of a posthumous son brought up by a witch grandmother to avenge an equally famous father killed at war by his own compatriots to spite their idiot king, his brother. But the hero over-reaches himself in the course of his quest for vengeance, and in a turn of dramatic irony that knocks one over, he just narrowly misses his doom at the hands of Smallpox. In its roll-call of characters, range of action, and tone of poetry and colour, this is classic drama we have shot on film and which we hope will show beyond the shores of Ijaw.

So much for the various kinds of traditional drama. Now how many are there of the type we have called modern? Two, if our count is correct. One is the folk theatre of Hubert Ogunde, Kola Ogunmola, Duro Ladipo and their several imitators, and the second is what some have called literary drama. Some would say the latter has its heart right at home here in Nigeria and its head deep in the wings of American and European theatre. The works of Wole Soyinka and my own plays, I am told, clearly bear this badge, but whether of merit or infamy it is a matter still in some obscurity. Of the former kind, however, Chief Ulli Beier, writing lately for *Nigeria Magazine* under the assumed name of 'Critic', is pleased to echo British opinions that *Oba Koso* by Duro Ladipo is representative of 'a new art form . . . neither opera, nor ballet nor poetic drama but all the three perfectly fused together'.

The emphasis in the above statement really ought to be on the fusion process, for the fact is that music, dance, and poetry have been the constants of true Nigerian drama from the earliest birth-marriage-and-death-cycle ceremonies and rituals to our own trials by error of today. The traditional theatre of sacred and secular dramas we have tried to outline here, from the ancestral to the epic plays, really is this 'closely unified combination of the arts' lost to Europe and America a long time ago. The difference has been in the variation, that is, the degree of the mixture these vital elements to drama undergo from play to play, place to place, each according to the purpose motivating the act. Thus for most, the ascendant elements are those of music, dance, ritual, and mime, that of speech being subdued to a minimum. This minimal use of dialogue probably is due to the fact that a good number of these plays belong to some particular group or cult in society and therefore require a certain atmosphere and amount of secrecy and awe. Silence can be an active agent of this. And because there often is little speech between characters outside of the invocations and incantations, it is easy to dismiss many traditional pieces either as simple pageants and processions or at best as forms close to opera and ballet. The achievement then of the folk theatre of the Ogunmola and Ladipo kind is that it has found the happy means between these ancient constants and the much newer ones of overall speech and plot or lack of it demanded by modern theatre. They have invented no new form. The English translation of Duro Ladipo's plays by Chief Ulli Beier in fact shows these to be no more than simple poetic dramas dependent on the accumulated image and utterance realized on a linear progression. These are no different from others of their species. But in the Yoruba, when not stripped of their concomitant music, dance and ritual, the total effect is terrific and different, and for a white man who has seen nothing like that since Boadicea and the Valkyrie, the impact is like a clean knock-out.

Very likely, the so-called literary theatre of Nigeria is beginning to miss this complete identity of purpose and response enjoyed increasingly by the folk theatre in Yoruba. Its latest plays show a definite tendency towards this composite art of the folk theatre. *Kongi's Harvest* by Mr Wole Soyinka, Mr Frank Aig-Imoukhuede's *Ikeke*, and my own *Ozidi* provide concrete evidence for this view. Whether this is a deliberate adoption of a principle, and whether working in English as these playwrights do, they will succeed in wedding that medium to Nigerian drum, song and dance is another matter and one for their individual talents.

An aspect of Nigerian drama acclaimed by even those who do not as yet acknowledge the existence of this art so expressive of our culture is the wealth and variety of its masks, costumes, and make-up. Talbot at the turn of the century went lyrical over the fact. Today the apparatus, a super-admixture of the symbolic and the naturalistic, still inspires instant applause and awe in the Nigerian theatre, indigenous or imported. As against this is the minimum use of sets and props outside the ritual paraphernalia, a fact that is also well-known for giving imagination full play.

But two aspects not so well noted by many are the use of the interpolated exclamation in Nigerian drama and the regular phenomenon of 'possession'. One is the spontaneous, independent outburst of cheering, directed to group or self, by members of the audience and players themselves. Together with music and dance as well as common story, which are obvious properties shared by all, this provides the spectator with that direct means of participation in the production so remarkable in Nigerian drama. The other is the incidence of 'possession'. This is the attainment by actors in the heat of performance of 'actual freedom of spirit from this material world, a state of transformation which has been given the rather sniggering name of "possession" or "auto-intoxication" by those outside its sphere c influence and sympathy'. This phenomenon features regularly in secular plays, especially the masquerade kind. It was a constant cause of hold-ups in any filming of the *Ozidi* saga at Orua! And such is the fear of the possible danger an actor may cause himself and others, when in this state of complete identification with his role, that leading irate masquerades in Ibo and Ijaw are usually provided with leashes held back or paid out accordingly by attendants. Nor could that state be a totally passive one, for at that stage when as the Ijaw put it, 'things unseen enter the man', the actor may become a medium, a votary of some ancestor spirits or divine powers filling him with the gift of prophecy.

Quite tied up with this phenomenon is the observance of certain taboos in a number of plays within the Nigerian repertory. Thus priests and worshippers of Obatala must not eat certain meals, nor wear any dress other than white. Performance of sacred dramas like that of Oshagiyan at Ejigbo cannot just be fixed for any day of the week. It must fall within only those that are holy to the deity. In *Ozidi*, the storyteller/protagonist may not have anything to do with women in the course of the seven-day production! This seems to be a carry-over of habits from the character to the player, a practice perhaps also applicable to other parts and other plays subject to particular taboos.

Now what are all these in aid of? Why the precarious preparations so fascinating to old Talbot? Why the risk of observing taboos the breaking of which means punishment and possible death? In the conventional Western theatre, the life though hazardous, is led for pure commerce and entertainment. Nigerian theatre, that is, its modern department, naturally now inclines that way. But traditional Nigerian theatre, so very much part of the contour of life in this country, what functions does it fulfil? Let us return to Mr Robin Horton with whom we said we had a little bone to pick. 'The masquerade belies the easy and oft-heard generalization that in traditional West African culture there was no such thing as Art for Art's sake. For although its performance is intimately associated with religious activity and belief, here it is the religion that serves the art, rather than vice versa. It is possible that some studies of West African culture have not found art practised for its own sake, simply because they have not looked for it in the right direction. This brings us to the second point. In describing the masquerade performance, I took pains to stress that its central element was the dance, and that the apparatus of costume and headpiece filled a subordinate place in the whole. I also stressed that the sculpted mask was first and foremost an instrument for securing the presence of a spirit, and not something produced as a work of art. This in fact is true of Kalabari sculpture generally.' Mr Horton then goes on to sound a note of warning. 'Now it would be dangerous to generalize on the basis of this one example. But taken together with reports on some other West African cultures such as that of the Ibo, it does make one suspect that, at least in certain areas of West Africa, the dance overshadows sculpture, painting, architecture and literature as the leading traditional art.'

Mr Horton's area of reference is rather wide. But it is true as he says that there is pure art in these parts. Limiting ourselves to a more compact area as we have tried to do we can point straight at our popular Agbor dancers and several seasonal dances of the kind staged by the young everywhere in this country. Mr Horton, however, is unfortunate in his choice of illustration. The Ijaw masquerade, that of Kalabari included, has always served a religious purpose quite apart from its entertainment value. In every Ijaw settlement there is a corpus of masquerade for every age-group of men. This ranges from the toddlers in an ascending order to the grizzle-headed elders, the degree of religiousness being in direct proportion to the position each occupies in the age hierarchy. The virgin palm fronds girding the headpiece of the chief masquerade, the fences of similar fronds this masquerade cuts through in his initial passage, and the actual sacrifice of gin and cockerel his priest makes to it on the field of play, these certainly are conscious acts of worship without which there can be neither perform-ance for pleasure nor peace for the age-group. What is more, the chief masquerade of the eldest group to which all adult males eventually graduate provides in many places the centre for a prominent communal shrine. The Oguberi at Kiagbodo and the masquerade of Kikoru at Okrika are such gods sporting powerful priests and to whom members of the community are asked by oracles in times of trouble to send daily prayers and individual offerings. Mr Horton is therefore somewhat playing it down when he gives the Ijaw masquerade as an example of art practised for art's sake in West Africa.

Indeed, it is doubtful whether any of the examples we have given of traditional Nigerian drama serves such dilettante ends. First, as Mr Horton himself admits, the very myths upon which many of these dramas are based, so beautiful in themselves, serve to record the origins and *raison d'etre* of the institutions and people who own them. Secondly, dramas, like the Ijaw masquerade and Ullu ritual, represent spirits and gods which their worshippers seek to propitiate in the manner described by Frazer. They are therefore manifestations of a special religion. Thirdly, they serve a civic and social purpose by educating and initiating the young into the ways and duties of the community. In the process they help to knit together persons of similar background, giving them a common identity. Fourthly, as the historian Dr E. J. Alagoa pointed out, masquer-ade dramas foster good relations between members of one village and another. A people famous for their performance will always have spectators pouring in from everywhere to see their show. In other words, the mas-querade can in fact become a town's best advertisement. Fifthly, these dramas, whether sacred or otherwise, often provide the one occasion in the year that brings home all true native sons and daughters resident and scattered abroad. This is the occasion for thanksgiving, allowing celebrants the double opportunity to report home and show off whatever priceless possessions they have won from their labours abroad. Sixthly, some induce that state of mind when the spirit is temporally freed of its flesh shackles and the medium is invested with extra tongues that can foretell any imminent disaster and if possible, prescribe prevention. A seventh use that

Nigerian drama is put to is to be found in the Urhobo drama-dance udje which is a vehicle for social comment, satire and sheer spread of meaty gossip. And last but equally vital, like all good drama, the Nigerian one is robust entertainment. Can a critic, starved though like Oliver Twist, ask for more?

One aspect of this drama is still left to examine, that of language. It is a mixed blessing that no text exists of many of the several examples we have given of Nigerian theatre. Mixed blessing because it saves us on the one hand the trouble of proving any special point, while on the other, it under-lines the sad fact that there are such mines of material lying around to be dug up for our national enrichment. But it can be safely said that each traditional piece does pride to the language of its people at all levels of meanings such as T. S. Eliot outlined for poetry in the theatre. So we believe does the folk theatre, at present mainly in Yoruba.

The difficulty and controversy come when we move into the department of modern drama in Nigeria – drama that usually is first seen in print before it is seen on the stage. The dispute has to do with that irascible hobby-horse of scholars like my friend Mr Obiajunwa Wali who foresees a dead end to African Literature written in European languages. But I would not like now to be taken on such a John Gilpin ride! Can it be valid and authentic literature? asks Mr A. Bodurin in the *African Statesman*. He goes on with the voice of dogma: 'In literature content and expression determine each other so fundamentally that the validity and authenticity of a work suffers as soon as the native content is expressed in a foreign language. This dissociation of content from expression is partly responsible for the difficulty in appreciating Wole Soyinka's plays. I am strongly con-vinced that if *A Dance of the Forests*, the most intriguing of his plays, were written in Yoruba, much of the obscurity would disappear.' Now let me quote another piece of castigation, this time of me. 'The usual criticism of Mr Clark's plays is that he has not quite found the kind of verse suitable for the presentation of dramatic action. This is, in my view, a just criticism. It is probably not consoling to add that Shakespeare did not begin to write good dramatic poetry till 1599, that is, till his tenth year in the theatre. No one ever begins by tossing of masterpieces. The delineation of character which is one of the springs of dramatic poetry is naturally a late accom-plishment. One has to be much more than a gifted lyricist even to create ordinary dialogue that is resourceful, natural, and imaginative while dealing with the drab details which are bound to find their way into a play.' That is Mr Ben Obumselu reviewing my play *The Raft* (or was it Mr Soyinka's production of it?) in *Ibadan*. After citing a passage which he never stops to analyse, he romps home: 'Mr Clark has not, as a dramatist, been fortunate in the kind of poetry he has admired.' Like the big names he then proceeds to drop all over the place. 'The . . . actors found it difficult to decide whether they were uneducated Nigerian lumbermen who spoke English indifferently, or poetic personages to whom imaginative poetry came naturally. Occasionally, they strayed into pidgin English rhythms as lumbermen. I doubt whether Mr Clark considered this matter sufficiently.' Let me assure Mr Obumselu here and now that I considered the matter most sufficiently. The characters in *The Raft* and in other plays of mine are neither 'poetic personages' nor the kind of Cockney he has in mind. They are ordinary Ijaw persons working out their life's tenure at particular points on the stage. And they are speaking in their own voices and language to an audience members of whom they expect to reach with a reasonable degree of sympathy and conviction. At this point, I would like to quote a letter I wrote from America in 1963 on this very subject to Mr Gerald Moore: 'Education and class consciousness which presuppose and actually create levels of speech and language in European societies have, thank God, not done that havoc to the non-literary tongues like Ijaw. Style, imagery, etc., these are what tell one user of a language from another – not grammar or class; for we haven't that. And you very well know that all I consider myself is a letter-writer for my characters.'

In other words, the task for the Ijaw, and I dare say any Nigerian or African artist, writing in a European language like English, is one of finding the verbal equivalent for his characters created in their original and native context. The quest is not on the horizontal one of dialect and stress which are classifications of geography, society, and education. It is on the vertical plane of what the schoolmasters call style and register, that is, the proper manner, level and range of dialogue and discussion. And this is a matter of rhetoric, the artistic use and conscious exploitation of language for purposes of persuasion and pleasure. If in the process, there occurs no 'dissociation of content and expression' as Mr Bodurin puts it, and I understand that term to mean, say, the discussion of food prices by market-women in the jargon of biologists, but on the contrary there is a faithful reproduction of the speech habits of one people into another language as Mr Chinua Achebe does significantly in English with the Ibo dialogue proceeding by technique of the proverb, then I think the artist has achieved a reasonable measure of success.

In this connection, I would like to draw attention to the use of another language device, that of indirection which features prominently in my own play *Song of A Goat*. That doctor and patient in that play do not approach the business on hand with the directness of an arrow does not mean the playwright is unappreciative of the importance of speed and despatch. Rather, it is a recognition by him of a living convention observed among the people of the community treated in the play, namely, that you do not rush in where angels fear to tread for the simple reason that the flying arrow either kills promptly or sends the bird in flight. Accordingly, delicate issues are handled delicately by these people. This approach is evident in their manner of negotiating marriage between one family and another and of announcing the news of death to the persons most affected. Each subject is tackled by indirection.

This is not to say the Nigerian playwright and novelist writing in English will not sometimes use the old gradation of speech as understood by all of us from our reading of European literature. Indeed some do use pidgin, like Mr Wole Soyinka in his play *Brother Jero*, Mr Cyprian Ekwensi in his novel *Jagua Nana*, and Mr Chinua Achebe in his latest terrifyingly prophetic and exact story *A Man of the People*. But the character using pidgin must be in a position to do so in actual life, and there must be a special purpose served. That is, there must be propriety. Thus the houseboy will speak to his master in our new urban social set-up in the pidgin that his education and class dictate. Similarly the Warri market-woman selling to a cosmopolitan clientele will use the pidgin that really is the lingua franca of that section of the country. In Mr Wole Soyinka's *Brother Jero*, however, the disciple Chume oscillates between 'pidgin' and the so-called standard or Queen's English. The excuse might be that at one time the situation demands that he speaks straight in English that is Pidgin English as befits an office messenger, while at another it requires him to speak in his original Nigerian tongue here translated into appropriate standard English as we have said.

Well, there it is; but will it do for the critics? One of them, I think Mr Bodurin, actually repeats the advice Mr Harold Hobson of the London *Sunday Times* was kind enough to give modern African playwrights free of charge, to wit, let them forget they have been to university. Perhaps, the critics should first take that advice! At the moment, many of them are encumbered with conventions and critical theories that pile up good grades in the old English schools, but then are thoroughly good for nothing thereafter. This is why, like the foreign 'rigorous teachers who seized their youths', these Nigerians require the special aid of programme notes setting out all strange practices as in Chinese theatre. But then it is the lot of artists to be often misunderstood.

Nadine Gordimer

▼▼▼▼▼▼▼▼▼▼▼▼▼▼▼▼▼▼▼▼▼▼▼▼▼▼▼▼▼▼▼

The Novel and the Nation in South Africa
[1961]

THE novel and the nation in South Africa – it's a nice tidy-sounding title, but what does it really mean? It implies a philosophical rather than a literary view of the novel, of course. It is significant, too, of the fact that the yardstick by which a book is measured in South Africa is often that of political rather than literary force. What is called for by such a title is not a piece of literary criticism so much as a consideration of how the novel has affected the South African people, and how the people have affected the novel.

I speak as if my subject has chosen me, rather than I it. And perhaps it has. 'Put your hand right in, into the very depth of human life! Everyone lives by it, but few know it, and wherever you grasp it, there it is interesting!' Goethe wrote this, Turgenev quoted it, and I believe it, as every writer must. But is it strictly true that a writer is limited only by the length of his reach? Aren't there all sorts of other influences that invisibly hold back his arm? Has he, as a human being in a particular time and situation, always the freedom of his talent? I do not speak of censorship, of the Pasternaks of this world, but of those who are limited even by the very necessity to speak out while they can, and by the interpretation of an atmosphere that fills their lungs and leaves no breath for further exploration. When I began to think about writers in my own country, I saw that the reasons why many of them have written as they have are centred more in the social situation they share than in their individual differences of talent and temperament. The way to approach them is with the long shot, to come upon them in the crowd, the fifteen millions among whom they live.

What is this crowd? At its simplest, of course, it is composed of South Africans like myself, my family, friends, acquaintances, co-citizens and so on, in wider and wider circles, until the entire fifteen million inhabitants of South Africa are enclosed in the concept. We are not an abstract concept, we breathe and are alive: yet, collectively, we ought to be more than the sum of ourselves, something other than ourselves. That other should be recognizable as our identity as the nation.

Now it is not likely that anyone, anywhere in the world today, who reads the newspapers is unaware of the political facts that make it impossible for South Africans to produce that super-identity at the present time. The world has become aware of us in the past ten or fifteen years, since the Continent of Africa began to change hands once more, this time from white hands to black, and the world is understandably mistaken in regarding our lack of a common identity as a condition of crisis. The fact is that never, at any time in the 400 years of recorded history in South Africa – not even in time of war with other nations – have we been able to produce that super-identity as a nation.

Reinhold Niebuhr, in his book *Nations and Empires*, makes a list of the forces of cohesion necessary to this identity. They are 'common language and a sense of ethnic kinship, geographic unity and contiguity, a common historical experience, and frame of political thought, a common area of economic mutuality, and, sometimes, the fear of a common foe'. Of these eight cohesive forces the people of South Africa can claim only two – geographic unity and contiguity and a common area of economic mutuality. We have no common language, and we have, of course, no ethnic kinship, but, on the contrary, a constant redefinition of quite ancient ethnic differences. Our common historical experience is not one of fighting together, but against one another – white man against black, Afrikaner against Englishman. We have no common frame of political thought, but a clash of bitterly opposed ideologies. As for fear of a common foe – the foe we fear is each other: the black man the political and economic domination of the white, the white man the black man's outnumbering him, and outbidding him for the world's support. It has never yet been possible for one of us to say, 'I'm a South African' as any American, for example, white, black or yellow, may say, 'I'm an American'.

If South Africans are not a nation, then what are they? What shall they call themselves, collectively? What is the nature of their life as social beings? What makes us hang – however loosely and angrily, like bees swarming on a telephone pole – together? Can we call ourselves a community or a collection of communities? Karl Jaspers, the German Existentialist philosopher, defines a community as follows:

> Community is a historical concept. Each separate community is unique, rooted in an unfathomable past that has determined it, and that has been handed down through oral teaching, books, usages, customs, habits, and, above all, through the institutions of the family and religion. Community

is something that grows, that cannot be planned; it may be preserved, but it cannot be created.

This description can scarcely be stretched to fit one of the gold-mining and industrial towns of the Witwatersrand, where the greatest concentration of white people live and are concerned with maintaining the *status quo* of white superiority, and where tens of thousands of black people are living through the extraordinary experience of an industrial revolution. These towns are cut in two as sharply as east and west Berlin, if for different reasons. The whites share neither oral teaching, books, usages, nor customs with the blacks, keeping to themselves the commonplaces of civilized life. The blacks have eagerly abandoned the tribal past and entered the workshop of the twentieth century, where that unfathomable past is stripped away and a man goes around naked while he puts together what patches and rags of the infinitely desirable present he can scrabble for.

The definition of a community would not fit, either, one of the artificial regroupings of black people in planned, segregated rural areas known as Bantustans which are at present being created. Neither would it fit one of the black townships where Johannesburg's immense labour force lives, and where the authorities impose ethnic division of the streets, so that the inhabitants of one row of houses may never forget the differences between them and their neighbours, instead of becoming aware of common cause with them. Johannesburg itself, white and black city, is not yet eighty years old, and though it has tremendous, clear-cut character of a kind unique on the African continent, it has no homogeneous substance from the past on which to draw. It is significant that no one even knows for whom it was named.

Jaspers' definition of a community does just fit, with minor adjustment, the rapidly vanishing life of an African kraal; it might have some bearing on an Afrikaans farming village, the sort of place whose physical isolation gave it the narrow homogeneity Pauline Smith wrote about in her wonderful short stories forty years ago. But for most of our fifteen millions the past began yesterday, the oral teaching comes from the commercial radio, the books are not about us, the only habit is the cinema and the only institution the Rugby game.

Now let us hear Karl Jaspers on his concept of 'society'. He defines society as a technological collectivity, and says it:

lives in the moment; it is not rooted in history, having no past; it is transferable at will, can be reproduced, can be charted, is the product of planning and can be created. 'Society' can replace any individual with any other, without changing its own character; it treats man as a means, as a part, as a function. It has no future save that of quantitative increase,

improvements in machines, replacements of men and materials which
have worn out with use.

That, to me, sounds more like South Africans and the way we live,
though it does not cover us altogether, and some of the things it lists are
goals we seem to be aspiring to for the future, rather than ways of life we
have achieved now. They are goals we share with the rest of the modern
world, for towards technological collectivity and away from the community
is the way the world is going; the big difference for us is that we have
never known the state of being a community – we seem destined to pass,
without ever having experienced the most fruitful and secure way of living
that the soul of man knows, directly from homelessness to regimentation.

This phenomenon must have the greatest possible influence on our
culture. For culture is not just an embellishment; it is the whole life of the
human spirit in communities: it is the means, and also, perhaps, the end,
of civilized living. Jaspers describes culture as the substance of the community; he says: 'Man's inner being is enriched as the substance present in
the community grows fuller; the creative individual is representative
of this substance, recognizing himself in its echo.'

At this point, then, the novelist and the nation bump into each other; the
creative individual and society meet. And in this meeting one sees that the
South African novelist has begun to create literature at a time in world
history when the community – the source of that substance of culture of
which a writer is one of the manifestations – is on the decline, and the
technological collectivity is taking its place. At the same time, he has grown
up in a society where 78 per cent of the population is cut off from the
normal cultural influences – libraries, art galleries, theatres and concerts –
by the colour bar, and the existing substance of culture is consequently
pitifully thin. Along with the South African poet, painter and composer,
the novelist has begun to be creative in uncreative circumstances.

I am aware that I offer this statement in apparent direct contradiction to
the popularly held belief that South African writing has received its
greatest impetus from something quite different. Conflict, they say, has
kicked us into print. Well, I don't deny it, and cannot, with the evidence
there to see on every publisher's list in America and England. Conflict can
provide a deep and powerful stimulus, but a culture as a whole cannot be
made out of the groans and sparks that fly. And it is out of a culture, from
which man's inner being is enriched as the substance in an integrated
community grows fuller, that a literature draws its real sustenance in the
long run. The thirst that comes from the salt of conflict will need some
quenching; Africa is a dry land in more ways than one.

The novelist in South Africa does not live in a community and has begun to write from scratch at the wrong time. Don't think I am patting down the red earth of Africa over his grave – I am not. He survives, and will survive, but the going is not easy for him. The word is prickly, but full of juice, like some of the plants of Africa, and the low cultural rainfall forces it to take on certain forms and shapes and not others. Although the English novel in South Africa is part of the great volume of writing in English, and, through that, gets caught up in the main trends of European and American tradition, there are certain kinds of novels, which, for the reasons I have just given, we are unlikely to be able to produce. While the novel in the outside world shows signs of moving this way, we are likely to find that we are moving there.

For example, one of the new group of French writers, Nathalie Sarraute, wrote recently that 'character is nothing other than a crude label he (the reader) makes use of . . . by way of convenience, for the purpose of orienting . . . his own behaviour'. She goes on to say that the French reader is too stuffed with facts about himself, he has been 'learning about too many things'. She says away with Balzacian detail, with who ate what for supper, and le Père Goriot's accounts, and whether there was a button missing on his waistcoat. The French reader knows all that, the trappings of 'character' are as fixed in his mind as the dress of the fairy queen or the wings of the angel. Madame Sarraute suggests that the trend is to clear the novel of the device of 'characters' that obscures its true business, which is to bring the minds of writer and reader to grapple with each other. The writer's purpose, as she sees it, is to dispossess the reader and entice him, at all costs, into the author's territory.

Now I think that this is an exciting idea – leave the cinema and television to pap-feed authenticity, the most obvious level of reality, and let the novel take the reader into the world of the writer's ideas without any game of dressing them up. And I think it can be done – has, of course, been done – in a country such as France, with a great general cultural tradition. There it may be true that 'the reader has been learning about too many things'. In South Africa, in Africa generally, the reader knows perilously little about himself or his feelings. We have a great deal to learn about ourselves, and the novelist, along with the poet, playwright, composer and painter, must teach us. We look to them to give us the background of self-knowledge that we may be able to take for granted. Consequently the novel-in-depth – what one might call the 'pure' novel of the imagination – cannot be expected to flourish in Africa yet. We are still at the stage of trying to read ourselves by outward signs. To get at our souls, it may still be necessary to find out how we do our monthly accounts.

Yet there is one aspect of Mme Sarraute's vision of the novel that the South African novel fulfils completely; where, I believe, it goes beyond any other contemporary work. Mme Sarraute wants an intimacy between reader and writer. Well, an extraordinary and terrifying intimacy exists between writer and reader in South Africa. They walk, hand in hand, round a dark house scarcely knowing what they may discover together about their way of life.

This is the time, perhaps, to say a word or two about commitment, and get it over with. There are a number of things to be committed to in South Africa – colour groups, language groups, political groups, and so on – and to be committed to one is to find yourself in bitter opposition to one, or some, or all of the others. The novelist writes about what sense he makes of life; his own commitment to one group or another enters his novel as part of, sometimes the deepest part of, the sense he makes of life. If, on the other hand, the commitment enters the novel not as part of the writer's own conception of the grand design, but as an attempt to persuade other people – then the book is not a novel but propaganda with a story. For the novel does not say, 'This is what you must do' but 'This is what I have seen and heard and understood'.

It is a curious thing about propaganda in novels: the competent propagandist who merely makes use of the fact that a story provides a palatable way to present his propaganda usually succeeds in turning out a reasonably interesting book. But when a real novelist, one who has struggled with the strangeness of life, reached to the unexplored borders of the imagination, and taken us into the territory he has marked out of the unknown – when he decides for some reason or other to write propaganda-with-a-story, the result is likely to be unreadable. For this reason, if no other, I do not intend to discuss novels which seem to me to be propaganda-with-a-story.

The problem of Africa, the idea of Africa and what she stands for imaginatively; the mixture of the old legendary continent and the new one drawing its first breath when the rest of the world is tired – this abstract Africa is becoming an element of the spiritual consciousness of the peoples of the modern world. As Donne once could write of his mistress – 'O my America, my Newfoundland', so, today, the European or American can conceive of his Africa – not a physical concept of jungles and desert and wild beasts and black men, but a state of regeneration, an untapped source in himself to which he wants to find the dangerous way back; another chance for, perhaps, another, other civilization that draws its sustenance from very deep, very far back. This Africa is a fearful place, but in the danger lies the hope of virtue. This Africa is, of course, really only a new name for an old idea – man's deep feeling that he must lose himself in order to find himself. And this Africa has become so prominent in the subconscious of the world that it is beginning to have its own literature: last year I read an excellent novel about Africa written by a man who has never set foot there, and makes no bones about it. I am speaking of Saul Bellow's *Henderson The Rain King*: the Africa it creates is the Africa of the values in Mr Bellow's mind.

While the problems of Africa, in abstract, have had the effect, on people outside the physical sphere of Africa's influence, of expanding them, making them re-examine their moral and spiritual boundaries and find them too narrow, those same problems have had another response from those of us who actually live on the earth of Africa ourselves. Under the terrors of these problems, we have shrunk rather than expanded: instead of seeking new freedom for man's spirit, we have felt the accepted moral values of the civilized world too large and have changed them to contain us more rigidly and narrowly. A sense of space seems to have oppressed us in our souls as well as in our bodies; we have shut ourselves in.

The greatest single factor in the making of our *mores* in South Africa was and is and will be the colour question. Whether it's the old question of what the whites are going to do about the blacks or the new question of what the blacks are going to do about the whites, or the hopeful question of how to set about letting the whole thing go and living together, it still is *the* question. It's far more than a matter of prejudice or discrimination or conflict of loyalties – all things you can take or leave alone: we have built a morality on it. We have gone even deeper: we have created our own sense of sin and our own form of tragedy. We have added hazards of our own to man's fate, and to save his soul he must wrestle not only with the usual lust, greed and pride, but also with a set of demons marked 'made in South Africa'.

The first novel to reveal the morality South Africa has built on colour was Sarah Gertrude Millin's *God's Stepchildren*. Nearly thirty years later Alan Paton wrote another novel, *Too Late the Phalarope*, within the confines of the same morality. The two books are different in approach, since Mrs Millin is a conservative while Mr Paton is an impassioned liberal, but both novels accept, as a working condition, as it were, the validity of that morality, and are created entirely in terms of that morality.

In *God's Stepchildren* the Rev Andrew Flood comes to South Africa to work as a missionary among the Hottentots in the year 1821. He is a weak and unlikeable man – surely one of the most unattractive characters anyone has ever invented, which is a pity, because through him we are at once confronted with vital questions, questions South Africans are trying to work out answers to in their lives today, and we are at once aware that he won't be equal to them. Flood stands – however unworthily – for Christianity and the ways of Western civilization: he wants to take these things to the Hottentots, an aboriginal people of southern Africa, but finds something he hadn't thought of – they have their own rough equivalents of these concepts in their paganism and their tribal system. They are *not* empty, negative, open. In the lazy confidence of their dirt and dancing, the absolute confidence of their own environment, their own earth beneath their feet, they ridicule him in his earnest religious argument. We are given, the first of many remarkable things in this book, a study of that insidious process known as 'going native' – the spectacle of a man losing the support of the habits of a lifetime. Flood comes to the weary conclusion that 'to make them like himself, he had to make himself like them'. (By the way, I am sure that the irony of the idea that anyone might want to be like Flood is not unintentional.) Flood marries a Hottentot woman to prove his good faith to the Hottentots.

And it is here, only forty pages on, that the novel changes its character, moves out of the general morality and down into the particular morality of South Africa. For Flood has sinned. He has not sinned against his religion, no; he has taken his Hottentot woman in Christian marriage, but in terms of the morality of the country, which he accepts, he has sinned against his white race. From now on the entire book is pervaded by a sense of sin, a Dostoevskian sense of sin. The colour issue has become a moral issue. Flood has sinned against his whiteness, and we follow the course of the retribution that comes upon the heads of his four succeeding generations. What is merely unconventional – mixed marriage – has become sin. At the end of the book Flood's great-great-grandson, Barry Lindsell, who is what we would now call a play-white, in South Africa, makes the decision to give his life – not his flesh and blood, but all that makes life worth living to him – to atone for the original sin of his great-great-grandfather. But what has his ancestor done? Murdered? Swindled? Sold slaves? No: none of these. He has married a black woman.

Barry Lindsell does not want to give his life to revenge himself on the society that has punished him for his measure of black blood: neither does he want to give his life to the attempt to change the attitudes of that society. He cares little for the sin against humanity; he wants to atone for the sin against the white race. Nowhere in the entire book is there the suggestion that this sense of sin is tragically, ludicrously misplaced. It accepts without question the white South African tribal *mores*, the white tribal morality. Yet I do not think we must assume that the author subscribes to this morality, that it is, in fact, her own; her story exists within it because the story comes out of what she has drawn from the substance of the life around her.

The book accepts as a condition of life the morality within which it exists, but near the end there are three words, spoken by a minor character, that seem to come from outside. When Barry Lindsell confesses to his young English wife that he has black blood in him, she says, in surprised relief: 'Is that all?' The cat is out of the bag, indeed, for the nation and the novel. Is that all? Is that the stuff of sin? Is that the stuff of tragedy? And if it is, at what a curious disadvantage must it put South Africans with the peoples of other nations, whose writers are concerned with man's survival and the meaning of his life on earth. Yet this is the truth we have been reading about in *God's Stepchildren*; the South African kind of truth.

In terms of tragedy as the rest of the world knows it, there is a tragedy in Alan Paton's *Too Late the Phalarope* – the private tragedy of a man of fine instincts in conflict with an instinct that seems misplaced from some earlier, brutish existence. The writer takes care to endow his hero with noble attributes and virtues, and provides that he shall bring about his own downfall, thus fulfilling the classical conditions of tragedy, that the hero shall topple from a height, and that the fall shall be brought about by a fatal flaw in his nature.

Peter van Vlaanderen is a Greek-godlike young man with that flaw. It takes the form of lust, a terrible hunger of lust that, it is suggested (and as modern readers we require this sort of psychological explanation, though the Greeks would not have bothered), has grown out of all proportion to the rest of van Vlaanderen's nature through his father's stern suppression of the son's affectionate needs as a child. This lust takes as its object, as such passions tend to, someone outside the usual ken of the man's life – such a passion requires abasement as an element of its satisfaction, and this can most easily be found in a furtive association with someone beyond the sufferer's social pale. Peter van Vlaanderen's lust takes as its object, as that of many men has done before him, an out-of-work servant girl. But she is black. The colour problem makes of this lust of van Vlaanderen's something hideous and unnatural, rather than an unfortunate venture into infidelity on the part of a strictly-brought-up young man. In terms of a morality outside South Africa, what he does would involve him in a private struggle, a private hurt and unhappiness between him and the wife whom he loves, and some social disapproval: but within the South African morality what he has done is dragged down the scale of sin to match the evilness of Humbert Humbert's relations with Lolita.

Van Vlaanderen himself believes, like the Rev Andrew Flood, that he has committed a sin against his white race. He speaks of the law that forbids what he has done as 'the greatest and holiest of all laws' – and it is not only the letter of the law about which he is speaking, but its spirit, as it exists among his people. Again, not murder, not swindling, but the mingling of the blood is the greatest transgression. Van Vlaanderen regards his own lust not as lust, but specifically as something connected with black flesh. It is not the awfulness of lust that shocks and shames; but the awfulness of its object – a black woman. The moral focus of the book, like that of *God's Stepchildren*, is off-centre. Van Vlaanderen envies – I quote – 'with a deep envy, those to whom the touch of a black skin is abhorrent, even if it were to lift a sick or dying person'. 'To have such a horror is to be safe.' What is inhuman is a source of envy to him. Think of the implications of this! Which of course, is what Mr Paton is leading us to do.

In the end, van Vlaanderen's relations with the girl are discovered, and he is undone; and all the consequences of tragedy fall upon him. But the morality of the novel – the morality of South Africa – claims tragedy on the wrong count. The thunderbolt misses; the explosion, like the moral truth, is off-centre. For lust can be a tragedy for a man, but it is not a national disaster.

In *God's Stepchildren* there was a voice from outside that said detachedly, just once: 'Is that all?' In *Too Late the Phalarope* there are two voices that speak outside the accepted morality of the book and they are not detached at all. The police captain who arrests van Vlaanderen says: 'I know of an offence against the law, and, as a Christian, I know an offence against God; but I do not know an offence against the race.' And when all normal ties of love and affection prove less strong than shame, and Peter van Vlaanderen's father closes his door to his son, and his wife is sent away back to her parents, the old aunt who has narrated part of the book says: 'The truth is that we are not as other people any more.'

There are many books that reveal South Africans to themselves as they have become, but I suppose, in the context of the novel and the nation, we ought to take a look at at least one historical novel that attempts to show us how South Africa got started off that way. The trouble with historical novels is that one is always conscious of the wardrobe mistress, hovering about in the background and tiptoeing over to adjust a wig or set a spear straight, just when one of the characters seems about to open his mouth and say something important. Anyway, let's try to ignore her. Peter Abrahams' *Wild Conquest* is one of the few novels that try to go back to the beginning of the great moral dilemma of black and white. In his story Peter Abrahams (who is himself a black South African) shows how a double burden of savagery and guilt on the part of both black and white bred hatred, and he takes as his starting point the day when the British decreed the freeing of slaves. Out of fear, the Boer masters of a band of black men who have been their slaves precipitate killing of both black and white. The slaves had intended to leave peaceably the land they had tilled and the homestead that they had built for their masters. But the Boers fear that their ex-slaves will try to take the farm and homestead, as has happened elsewhere, and they kill one of the slaves as a gesture; there is a fight and the Boer family leaves to join the Great Trek to the hinterland, away from the jurisdiction and administration of the British. They set the homestead on fire behind them.

This novel gives us, too, an idea of what the trek meant to the forebears of those who make up the great majority of the nation – the Africans themselves. The wise man of the Matabele says that the coming of the white man deep into the interior meant 'the end of living by the spear and the beginning of living by the head'. The book ends at the great clash between black and white, when the Matabele were defeated. It is 'the point between yesterday and tomorrow. The old ends here; the new starts here. This is the end of a lifetime. The beginning of a lifetime.'

The two books written within the accepted framework of the South African morality that we had already discussed before our excursion into the past – *Too Late the Phalarope* and *God's Stepchildren* – are part of what one might call the literature of victims. This is, by the nature of the social structure there, quite a considerable literature in South Africa. We are shown what people suffer under the imposition of a particular policy, a way of life, a particular morality. There are no, or few, pictures of the law-makers, the politicians and leaders themselves; neither are the victims shown in anything but a passive role – what is done to them, rather than how they take it, is the subject-matter of the book. *Episode*, by Harry Bloom, is a novel about how they take it, and more grimly, how they give it back. Peter Abrahams' *A Wreath for Udomo* goes a step further, and is about the sort of problems ex-victims have to face when they are freed of an imposed system, and have to work out a discipline and morality of their own. Both these novels are about people totally submerged in an event: Mr Bloom's about the mass from which the people find their leaders; Mr Abrahams' about the leaders once they have arisen. Both are highly relevant to what is happening now on one part of the African continent or another, but Mr Bloom's is the one that speaks of what is happening on our part of the continent, to us, the people among whom I live. And when I say us, I mean just exactly that – all of us of all colours who live in South Africa, not the mutually exclusive 'them' and 'they' of our daily lives within the South African caste system.

Episode is about a riot in a Transvaal small-town location. The riot begins with the loss, by a washerwoman, of a white man's shirt-collar; no one has suggested a second's suspension of belief in the book over this – as a people we are all aware that peace may be broken by a beer-mug in our country. Somewhere in the first chapters one of the characters in the book says to another, 'Tell me, do the people here do much wishing?' And the answer is 'Yes, but they don't wish hard enough. . . .' The novel sets out to show, with the determined realism of a Zola, a tragic way in which people may be carried over from the state of wishing to the state of action.

Wishing does not plan, it merely summons the blind force of the will, sprung from the lamp full-grown and terrible. The people whose genie it is do not know what to do with it once it is let loose.

Episode is the novel of the political man; he has few private emotions and problems. The location does not belong to the old homogeneous community of the black man, either, but to the technological collectivity of modern South Africa. It is the world of the white man that the black man has entered by socio-economic means, his need of work and the white man's need of his work, instead of by the mingling with a white man's blood as in *God's Stepchildren*. The factory door and not the womb provides the entry to Harry Bloom's world.

The Africans in *Episode* are social beings, thinking people; they have other qualities than the patience, endurance and acceptance of the stock African in our literature. We see in them not so much a picture of the past decaying in the present as of the present feeling for a future. That the form this takes in the story is a hideous, senseless riot does not mean that the theme is obscured. When these people yell *Mayibuye* – Africa, may it come! – the thinking ones are well aware of the dilemma that freedom could bring. Paul Mabaso, an ex-soldier, now an African Congressman, wonders: '. . . if it came in his time, what part would there be for him? Would it not need other types of men; engineers, administrators, educators? Would not the embattled, scarred, exhausted men find themselves aliens in the world they had created?'

There is no shame at being black in this book; but neither is it suggested that there is some special virtue in a black skin, in the way that there is a special virtue in whiteness within the South African morality, and I do not think there is any particular significance in the fact that it was written by a white man rather than a black one. We all await with tremendous interest the novels to come from the twelve millions who, with only one exception I can think of, have not yet written any novels in English – which it seems almost certain is destined to be their literary language. But I do believe that we should await these books as an appeal to the intellect and imagination rather than to curiosity. For that is the true business of the writer, to appeal to the intellect and imagination; the satisfaction of curiosity properly belongs to the newspapers. Below the level of the meretricious satisfaction of curiosity – how it all looks to someone who really *is* black – there is little reason why a straightforward novel of events in which the protagonists are black men should not be written just as authentically by a white writer as by a black one. Just so long as he makes it his business to know the social forces that shape his protagonists, as the writer who writes of men at sea must know the sea.

The novel in depth, the novel that is not authentic but imaginative, that does not seek to create the semblance of life but to create life out of its own elements – that, perhaps, can be written of the black man only by himself. But even of this we cannot be sure.

It is a great pity that, with the exception of the novels by Peter Abrahams, there are no English novels written by black Africans for us to discuss, although there is a growing volume of black South African writing generally, and if short stories and essays came within our scope, it would be different. Unfortunately, black Africans in South Africa who are beginning to write now seem to put the material that we might hope to see used in novels into biographies. It is partly the temptation to satisfy that need of our nation and other nations who are interested in us – the need of curiosity. It is partly out of the writer's fear of the different and greater demands made by the creation of a novel. But it is a pity, because if that material of living were to be transposed, we should be given the extra dimension of the novel – the dimension that makes it possible for us to know all, if the novelist chooses to tell us, about the minds and souls of the people in the novel, that extra dimension that gives us, in fact, the freedom of the city of the writer's imagination. Freed of the inhibition of telling his own story and that of those who impinge upon it, the writer would have a better chance of giving us what we really want him to cull from his experience of living – what sense he makes of life. He would take more from and add more to that watery substance which is the culture of South Africa. I think that black African writers will have to take care not to take advantage of the easy opportunity to use their talents to satisfy curiosity; this sort of writing, however interesting, may make a competent journalist, but does not make a creative writer. And if a man has it in him to create, he should not squander the stuff of his experience.

Many South African novels draw their force from the fact that they are written from the standpoint of one particular situation, and it is unlikely that while you are within the stockade thrown up around your mind by the situation about which you are reading, you will be aware that a common ground runs from under your feet to beneath the stockade of another particular situation, and another. Take *God's Stepchildren* and *Episode*, for example – where is the piece of common ground on which, once the stakes were pulled up, they would be found to be resting? I should say that it would be among the stunted bushes of Dan Jacobson's Karroo – the Karroo is the semi-desert sheep-farming country of the Cape Province. Jacobson's Karroo is a ground of doubt and questioning. He is one of a few writers (I am one of them myself) who in the past ten years have written of the gaps and uncertainties and ambiguities of being a South African – mostly of being a white South African, though, by an oblique but eloquent technique, also of being a black South African. If, at worst, to paraphrase Yeats, these writers lack conviction, then at least they escape the apoplexy of passionate intensity that bedevils the country.

The point of Jacobson's sort of novel is that it does not slap on to common experiences in South African life the given, easily recognized trade-mark, but shows them happening; the category into which they must fall, as experiences must be decided, re-thought-out by us, the readers. The writer cannot really describe them; he has absorbed them from the day of his birth, and the process of his becoming conscious of them is the actual stuff of the book. This is what I feel; what is this? he says. There is a terrifying lack of pretence in his books. He does not accuse us, but there are times when we cannot look him in the eye. There is the sudden guilt of knowing what he's getting at better than *he* knows. . . . He does not teach or instruct; he goes further, he illuminates.

Jacobson's white man in Africa is not a towering bully or a willing sacrifice in the historical cause of bringing Africa into the twentieth century. The burden of politics is the ball of dung he's struggling to push up the hill; but around him are 'heat, distance, the difficulties of poverty and ignorance' – man's fate, black or white, in Africa. South Africans are always prattling about the things that know no distinction of race, or creed, or colour. Well, here they are, and they are not only freedoms that we have yet to win. There is a struggle that we are all in together, already committed to whether we know it or not. Mr Jacobson's young medical student in *A Dance in the Sun* says of himself and his fellow-countrymen:

> A multi-coloured nation of nomads we seemed to be, across a country too big and silent for us, too dry for cultivation, about which we went on roads like chains. We were caught within it, within this wide, sad land we mined and did not cultivate.

This same young man explores the special loneliness of South African life, the loneliness of all of us, black and white and any-coloured, in our society which is not homogeneous, not integrated, where the whites are de-Europeanized and the blacks are detribalized, both are cut off from each other by the colour bar, and there is no community. Mr Jacobson's student calls this loneliness a 'kind of homesickness . . . but it was a sickness for a home I never had, for a single cultivated scene, for a country less empty and violent, for people whose manners and skins and languages were fitted peaceably together'. We are out of the world of political concepts, and down to the facts of human needs.

The two students in *A Dance in the Sun* are young liberals who find themselves with the conventional situation of a black man wronged, without hope of redress, by a white man and his family. They resolve to help the wronged man, and in the course of doing so they find out one or two things about the white liberal attitude, and the difficulties it presents in practice. We are shown that it is the liberal attitude – the no-colour-bar one – that is crude and untried in South Africa; whereas the *intrinsically* crude relationship of the black-man-in-his-place, the white-man-in-his – 'that is mellowed, that is history'. There is self-examination of liberal motives, too; the kind of self-examination that liberals are often discovered, by the more radically-minded, to be avoiding. The young men's chance to help Joseph against his white oppressors is not only to be taken as the necessity for one human being to help another or even in the name of cold justice. 'Guilt and pity were hunting us out of the country,' one of the young students admits. 'Here was an opportunity to expiate both.'

Some novelists interpret what we say and do out loud – Mr Jacobson overhears us in our sleep – but William Plomer and Olive Schreiner seize upon and decode those symbols that even in our dream disguise from us our deepest selves. William Plomer published *Turbott Wolfe* in 1925, a year after *God's Stepchildren* was published, so it's reasonable to presume that these two books were being written at about the same time. I mention this because it is a good example of the irrelevance of chronology when one is considering novels and novelists – *Turbott Wolfe* with its talk of African nationalism and its view of Africa as a black man's country would seem the sort of novel of South African life far more likely to be written now than in the 1920s. But Plomer wrote his novel culled from the life he felt around him and thought out for himself; he saw what that life was, in its essence and therefore its potential, instead of writing about it according to pre-arranged concepts and the shape it was squeezed into by the South African morality. He was not a prophet but a fearless thinker whose imagination took a leap.

Turbott Wolfe himself is not a South African, but an Englishman. He plunges into Africa from without: he has not absorbed and breathed in the attitudes of morality of South Africa from birth, as Dan Jacobson's students have. He does not come, either, like the Rev Andrew Flood, to preach and teach; he is free, and he has quite a lot in common with Henderson, the big, life-greedy American in Saul Bellow's book, who journeys through a spiritual Africa in search of the meaning of man's life.

At the outset, when Wolfe goes to run his trading store in Zululand, he considers the colour business as something to be decided by the individual himself: 'There would be the unavoidable question of colour. It is a question to which every man in Africa, black, white or yellow, must provide his own answer.' *God's Stepchildren* would not grant this; *God's Stepchildren* says: this is the way it is, black here, white there; you transgress at your peril and there is no suggestion that there might be something of the gains of honour and decency in the transgression.

Turbott Wolfe does not measure Africa against the white man, but the white man against Africa. He presents the reverse side of that attitude of which the obverse is the repellence of the black skin – he is fascinated by blackness. This fascination is again given to us in its most obvious and basic form – he is attracted by a black girl. So was Peter van Vlaanderen, and, like van Vlaanderen, Wolfe finds the attraction is 'something he hadn't bargained for'. He is not unaware of the social and legal consequences of such an attraction, but he has *no sense of crime or sin*. 'I was afraid of falling in love with her,' he says; and, with those words, the whole matter of sexual relations across the colour line is lifted out of the back yard and into the front bedroom, so to speak. It forces us to admit something that, within the South African morality, is unthinkable, something that even those South Africans who do not accept the *dicta* of that morality tread delicately round and tacitly ignore. Sexual relations between black and white are like any other; there is always the possibility of love. And love with its wider connotations of respect and loyalty and unselfishness, of its honoured place in the family and the community, everyone knows belongs to the higher manifestations of the human spirit. It is difficult, indeed, to equate these manifestations with sin. We need not believe in, indeed we can quite easily find grounds to laugh at, the pretext of Turbott Wolfe's feelings for Nhiliziyombi, the black girl, who is more noble savage than woman, lyrically described as 'an ambassadress of all beauty – it might be called holiness, that intensity of the old, wonderful, unknown, primitive African life' and so on – but the moral challenge has been flung down.

The novel forces us to face the rightness or wrongness of an attitude, in principle, but it does not suggest that facing a matter of this kind, in principle, solves its problems in practice. In fact, it admits that this is only the beginning.

The emphasis of the novel is contained in Turbott Wolfe's desire to find people who are 'frank and open in a country full of deceit'. The novel itself, made of the ordinary elements of life in South Africa, but truer and larger than life, standing for the life we live there, rather than bothering to simulate it, shirks nothing. One by one the hypocritical concepts of Africa invented by the white man, political, economic, sexual and social, fall, and it is certain that if *Turbott Wolfe* were being written today it would bring the hypocritical concepts of Africa that are presently being invented by some black men crashing down just as splendidly. Mabel van der Horst says, 'What the hell is the native question? You take away the black man's country, and shirking the consequences of your action, you blindly affix a label to what you know the black man is thinking of you. Native question indeed. . . . It isn't a question. It's an answer.'

And so we come last to the first South African novel – the chronological form of order is not, I think, anyway, the one best suited to the consideration of writers, who dart about in time, the best because they have the prescience of imagination – the present is not enough for them – the lesser because they cannot interpret the character of their contemporary situation and so see it in terms of the ready-made, ready-thought-out conceptions of the past – the present is too much for them. In this particular case, what appears to be merely defiance of chronology is in fact the greatest homage the present can pay to the past. *The Story of an African Farm*, written by Olive Schreiner and published in 1883, is not something over and done with; it is instead the sort of novel we can hope is to come. Its quality is best defined in the words of the stranger in the book itself, who says of the wood-carving the boy Waldo makes for his father's grave '. . . the whole of the story is not written there, but it is suggested . . . the attribute of all true art, the highest and the lowest, is this – that it says more than it says, and takes you away from itself.' The eye of Olive Schreiner's consciousness opens on a Karroo farm in the 1870s but it takes us away to nothing more limited than the mystery of life itself. The other novels we have been considering have attempted to answer the question 'What does a man make of life in South Africa?' This one attempts to answer the eternal question: What is the life of man? The answer is presented like one of those frost flowers that in their slight, brief beauty contain a pattern that is one of the fundamental forms of the universe itself.

The freedom that Lyndall, one of the two central characters, burns for – it is not freedom from the colour bar, but freedom for women in an age when independence for women was an issue. But what does it matter? All oppressions are the same in their effect on the oppressed, and what she suffers is valid for all who suffer a man-imposed limit on the scope of their minds and bodies, is of the nature of such suffering itself. And the spiritual progression of the boy Waldo, struggling to understand himself and the relation of man to his godhead, alone and ill equipped – a poor, ignorant boy 'so blinded by thinking and feeling that he has never seen the world' – that same struggle is being lived through by many young Africans in the black townships today, and by those young people of all colours who ask some meaning of a life that provides, at best, for the senses but not for the searching mind, not even to the extent of furnishing the cultural means of going about the search.

This novel has a special significance in that itself it provides one of those cultural means: it stimulates intellectual curiosity, something conspicuously lacking in South African culture, almost lost to us through our preoccupation with our own social and political problems. 'I like to realize forms of life utterly unlike mine,' says Lyndall. And restlessly, tirelessly, through

Lyndall and Waldo, who together make up the questing nature of life itself, we explore nature and the nature of man, in this book. Olive Schreiner has none of the intellectual timidity that would make her limit herself to the things she knows, the little world she knows. She is not afraid to make pronouncements, her own definitions of the great and ineluctable. The book is full of guesses at the things we want to know, the questions at the centre of existence with which we are all always concerned at that level where our lives plunge out of grasp. She analyses the nature of work of different kinds, and what it does to and for men; she ponders on crime and identity, and on genius. The novel is glorious with irrelevancies, for nothing is irrelevant to the exploration of life, and Lyndall and Waldo are in exploration of life. That is their purpose; true innovators, they are taking it as far as it can go, rather than trudging from one of the accepted human goals to another – love, work, success, salvation – as people do in most novels.

'Truth begins in dialogue,' said Nietzsche. What the South African novel is doing at present is making heard that dialogue. *The Story of an African Farm* is always there to remind South Africans that though they may have changed and shaped themselves according to the laws and ideals within their particular situation, and though their novel does and of necessity must concern itself with making sense of what has happened to them, they have not contracted out of the wider human condition. In the end the question they must ask of the novelist, and the one he must attempt to answer is: What is the life of man?

APPENDIX

This essay was written as the Anne Radcliffe Memorial lecture, given at Harvard in 1961. Although the main thesis holds good for me, and indeed has been confirmed by a decade that has seen increasing fragmentation of South African society, a great many changes have taken place that either have or – more significantly – have *not* been reflected in contemporary South African writing. I did not mention my own work in this essay; there were novels tackling the same sorts of themes that I felt I could discuss more objectively. But if I had been writing in 1972 instead of 1961 I should have had to include some consideration of my own novels, since I am one of the very few South African writers – all white – who have dealt in the dimension of imaginative writing with the motivation of events such as the sabotage attempts of the middle sixties, the shadow world of underground political activities, and the big political trials. Mary Benson (*At The Still Point*), Jack Cope (*The Dawn Comes Twice*), and I (*The Late Bourgeois World*), wrote novels with these realities as our background; all three were banned. I think I am the sole example of a South African who has chosen that other new theme – the decline of a liberalism, black-and-white, that has proved itself hopelessly inadequate to an historical situation.

Why have these pressing themes not been tackled by black writers? (And will they not write, either, of the present rise of black separatism as opposed to the sort of separatism imposed by whites?) This brings us to the other big changes since 1961: the introduction of the Censorship Act in 1963, and a few years later, the ruthless total banning of the written or spoken word of virtually all prominent black South African writers – Ezekiel Mphahlele, Lewis Nkosi, Alex la Guma, Dennis Brutus, for example. This last measure has been intimidating, to say the least, for aspirant black writers; and combined with awareness of the powers of the censors, not so much to ban individual books as to draw unwelcome official attention to the individuals who have written them, produced a long silence. It can scarcely be said to have been broken by the appearance of occasional stories by young black writers who for the most part wrote as timidly or penny-dreadfully as if Can Themba – first exiled, then dead – had never flourished a sharp pen out of Sophiatown. Since Alex la Guma went into exile there has been no novel of any worth written by a black in South Africa. Bessie Head's *Where Rainclouds Gather* and Ezekiel Mphahlele's *The Wanderers* are novels of exile by exiles.

But the silence of black writers has been broken, at last, by the very recent emergence of a number of young blacks writing – not novels, not criticism, not stories, but poetry. Oswald Mtshali, the first black poet to have a collection published in South Africa since Vilakazi, is the best known; there are also Wally Mongane Serote, Stanley Motjuwadi, Njabulo Ndebele, Mandlenkosi Langa and Pascal Gwala. No new white novelists or story writers of more than mediocre interest have emerged either (the only outstanding prose talent is the playwright, Athol Fugard), but there are, again, a number of interesting young white poets. The explanation for a new poetry, new poets? I can only offer – though not entirely convinced – a quotation from Nadezhda Mandelstam's *Hope Against Hope*, referring to poetry in the Soviet Union: 'Poetry does indeed have a special place in this country. It arouses people and shapes their minds. No wonder the birth of our new intelligentsia is accompanied by a craving for poetry never seen before – it is the golden treasury in which our values are preserved; it brings people back to life, awakens their conscience and stirs them to thought. Why this should happen I do not know, but it is a fact.'

C

The changes in life in South Africa since 1961 would lead me to quarrel with one statement I made confidently at the time of writing my essay. I remark there that 'there is little reason why a straightforward novel of events in which the protagonists are black men should not be written just as authentically by a white writer as a black one. Just so long as he makes it his business to know the social forces that shape his protagonists . . . etc.' I now believe that Georg Luckacs is right when he says that a writer, in imaginative creation and the intuition that comes with it, cannot go beyond the *potential* of his own experience. That potential is very wide; but living in a society that has been as deeply and calculatedly compartmentalized as South Africa's has been under the colour bar, the writer's potential has unscalable limitations. There are some aspects of a black man's life that have been put impossibly beyond the white man's potential experience, and the same applies to the black man and some aspects of a white man's experience. Both can write of the considerable fringe society in which black and white are 'known', in a meaningful sense, to one another; but there are areas from which, by iron circumstance, each in turn finds himself shut out, *even intuitively*, to their mutual loss as writers.

Finally, I quoted Nietzsche in my essay: Truth begins in dialogue. No need to point out, from hindsight, that it was not the kind of dialogue sought after by Mr Vorster that I had in mind.

Cheikh Hamidou Kane

▼▼▼▼▼▼▼▼▼▼▼▼▼▼▼▼▼▼▼▼▼▼▼▼▼▼▼▼▼▼▼▼

The African Writer and his Public
[1966]

T HE decision to make African literature a subject of study at
university level is the crowning event in its history. This decision
was taken at the Congresses of Negro Writers and Artists held in
Paris and Rome[1] and at the colloquiums held in Dakar under the patronage
of the Arts Faculty and in Freetown at Fourah Bay College. The increasing
number of translations of the works of Negro writers and the awards they
have received throughout the world are proof of the esteem in which our
writers are held and bear witness to the remarkable vitality of their work.

A more careful study of the present stage of our literature leads us to a
conclusion quite unlike the above, however. Quite a few people are even
ready to say things have reached a highly critical stage brought about by
the need to renew old themes and adapt our literature to a new post-
colonial era. The African writers who came together at the congresses in
Paris and Rome understood quite clearly that, in the struggle against
colonialism, against a colonialism that no longer needed to prove its
intention of staying in Africa eternally, it was their duty to take part in this
fight by putting their art at the service of their people. They showed their
awareness of this fact by declaring, in a communiqué issued after the
Conference of African and Asian Writers held in Tashkent, that they were
'fully aware of the need of freedom in order to create anything of literary
value'.

At these different congresses, our writers showed their readiness to
become fully *engaged* – a readiness which was to affect the orientation of
African literature since the writers wished to avoid all gratuitousness in art
and were ready to fight colonialism in all its forms until it would be wiped
out for good as far as their country was concerned. This explains why the
works of recent years reflect so very clearly the authors' satirical intention
which we see in impassioned writing and fine irony. This was a determining
choice – that of working towards a literature that would bear witness to the

[1] Organized by *Présence Africaine*.

times – and which meant that adequate means would have to be found in order to do this, namely, through realism. The articles many of our writers wrote justifying this choice give food for thought, many of them ending in an apology for Soviet realism! However, the independence of a number of African States is now a fact, a fact that became reality far sooner than anyone expected. No one thought colonialism was really dead – and this politically-angled literature is no longer in vogue. In the form defined by the various congresses, it can have no object; it is anachronistic and overhung with the aspirations of the public. An adaptation has become necessary; a certain alteration in the very line of progress shows itself to be inevitable.

The crisis people are talking about is the result of this situation; the result of the divorce between the objectives our literature has assigned to itself and African reality. Too taken up by the fight against colonialism, our literature seems to have lost sight of the need to prepare for the future: too conditioned by its involvement, it subordinated everything to it. The crisis it is going through now can be seen in the all too rare number of genuine literary works and in the silence of the 'great ones', often absorbed by political activities to the exclusion of everything else. Some critics think these tenors 'warble in secret'. It is obvious that our literature is still finding its way and is now at a crossroads. The present situation is the result of a crying need for new inspiration. A lot of old-time tenors seem to have had their day and change can be hoped for only through young writers who have not exhausted their talents in occupations which are souldestroying as far as art is concerned and have so far avoided a strict and superficial realism ruinous to any development.

A lot of the articles that have been written about the present stage of African literature show quite clearly that there are two schools of thought on the subject. The first groups those who avail themselves of the growing public anxious for more African literature and who give proof of indomitable optimism. This public is mainly European and this literature is almost exclusively addressed to them, as we shall see in a moment. The second school of thought (one rapidly winning many supporters) consists of those who are impatient at the slow rate of change, a change they all long for and which would make the writer direct his work towards Africa.

It is not our intention to examine the first position, to praise yet again the wealth and rich potentialities of our literature: the mere mention of Senghor, Birago Diop, Dadié and Oyono is enough. As to the second position which is becoming more and more usual among young critics anxious for authenticity and effectiveness, some of these are quick to speak not only of a critical stage but of bankruptcy. We feel this is going too far and too fast.

They maintain, with amazing unanimity, that the 'misfortunes' of African writers result mainly from the fact that they lack a public and that their work has no real grip on the African public for whom they claim to be writing. Between such a statement and the cry 'impostor' there is only one step needed . . . a step that has often been taken. Various warning signals ought to have put some people on their guard and let them expect a situation that more shrewder writers feared for some time. Some were very soon aware of the dual nature of their public – African and European – and of the different attitudes towards their work.

The two publics could not, nor can they now, react in exactly the same way to a literary work. They necessarily analyse it in ways which are utterly different from each other. This means that the writer, from the very start, has got to conciliate antinomic requirements, given the two contrasting types of reader. It was not possible for him to fully satisfy the needs of one without leaving out some aspects insisted on by the other. The struggle against colonialism, and also the encouragement given by European critics, was decisive to the direction African writing was to take. It also called for a painful choice. The African writers, with a beneficial sense of opportunism, decided to direct their action mainly towards Europe and the world outside Africa. The very nature of our literature, the conditions governing its birth and development are such that there is no choice. The solution found, in fact, was the only logical one. It is the consequences of this choice that concern us now and the gap which has begun to widen and separate the writer from his African public.

Let us first consider the circumstances which gave rise to this problem (some deny its very existence, whilst others think of it in terms that result from an understandable impatience). We shall try to show what are the new trends in African writing and analyse and justify the contrasting reactions of the two publics. The solution offered, if not original, is one calling for common sense and a strengthening of relations between traditional African writing and the new. In other words, for the new trends to be thoroughly embedded in a cultural reality which is African culture.

The problem facing Negro-African writers is an old one, but one highly relevant to the future of African writing. In rather special circumstances (now fortunately changed) it greatly contributed to the mature development of our writing but what is to be feared now is that it may force our writers to mark time until a solution is found. In one of the very first issues of *Présence Africaine*, Leonard Sainville went into the question very thoroughly, recognizing the difficult position the African writer is in and how much he suffers from the feeling of not being really understood by anyone. Europe expects from him something other than the message he is anxious to give, and he feels he has cut all links with his origins. Sainville defines the conditions which ought to contribute to the formation of a genuinely African public. 'Condemned, for the moment, to speak to a public scarcely apt to understand our claims and our hopes, we must, while holding the attention of this public and calling on our audience to show us understanding and the desire to understand, fight so that the other public, the public we are writing for, increases a hundredfold to become, in record time, an ideal public.'

The cry of alarm went up. The African writer has never had a public and he has always been conscious of the fact. Solutions offered by various people to speed up the awareness of the public could only be pious hopes in the colonial era. It obviously devolved upon the writer to turn to his people and make them 'concerned' by what he wrote. This was the solution recommended at the Congress in Rome and various communications reveal the increasing interest shown in matters relating to the writer-artist and his public. It was inevitable. This congress, like the one that preceded it, was an occasion for our artists and writers to examine their consciences and to situate themselves in true perspective as far as the fight against colonialism was concerned, as well as to take stock of their responsibilities towards their people. The last resolution passed on literature reflects this preoccupation which was to safeguard the genuinely African nature of our writers. A recommendation was made to 'form an African Theatre Group, and in so doing, not to disfigure African theatre'. With regard to poetry, the congress expressed the wish that 'the new content of Negro poetry in relation to Negro peoples and their different styles' should be determined. The congress called on our writers and artists – and the present state of our literature is a perfect illustration of the wisdom of such a position – 'to realize a harmonious synthesis of treasured tradition and modern forms of expression'. We must admit, alas! that such appeals, which received the unanimous vote usual on such occasions, have had little effect.

The importance of the problem can hardly escape the attention of Senghor the singer of negritude who, in his many articles, found many a felicitous phrase calling on his fellows to plunge into a bath of Africanity. When the majority of African States became independent, the problem took on a new aspect. The recovery of freedom and dignity that the Negro writer had given himself as an aim, meant that new perspectives were needed and a solution that would take into account the change of circumstances. The struggle against colonialism had to give place to taking part in building the city of the future. In front of the slow rate of change in the work of restoring its literature to Africa, the new criticism (new in its youth and its demands) showed its exasperation. This criticism no longer speaks the language of Europe or the university although the latter exists since it is to Lilyan Kesteloot that we are indebted for an excellent thesis on

African literature and to the concern of Roland Colin in his 'African Literature of Yesterday and Tomorrow' who both share the worry of Africans on this matter. This new criticism attracts the attention of the public by its tone, but also by an identity of views which precedes a penetrating analysis of the present state of our literature. In an article entitled 'La grande misére de la littérature Négro-Africaine' (*Jeune Afrique*, September 12, 1965), Signaté Ibrahima takes another look at the problem and calls for what he calls 'cultural decolonization'. 'In any case', he says, 'the writer has no real influence in his country. His public will be pretty sure not to know the language he is writing in. He is writing – Heaven defend us! – for Europeans! This is a fact, not an easy one to take. He is writing primarily and apparently without any afterthought, for a foreign public and it is in Paris that the laurels grow.' This attack would not have meant anything had it not been made again and again. In the review, *France-Eurafrique*, Urbain Dia-Moukori joins with Signaté in asking, 'And who are the Negro writers of the new generation writing for? There are far more novelists among them. . . . They want to show, to describe, to analyse situations. But who are they writing for? Who are they looking at and who are they hoping will listen to them? To read their work, I am of the opinion it is not Africans they hope will listen. They have not learned the literature of their people and the powerful flow of the collective unconscious refuses to pick up what they discard, and only casts it on to the riverbank like driftwood. They can go on saying they are not writing for anybody in particular. Their brothers are there observing them, waiting for what they produce.' The great differences in reasons put forward as to the underlying causes of the present crisis ought not to distract us from the main cause.

All these explanations come back to the dual public of the African writer and to the almost wholly exclusive orientation of his work towards Europe. The same cry is going up everywhere and there is general agreement as to the situation of the writer in search of a public. What is particular to our literature is that it hopes to satisfy two different publics. In every other country, what writers want most of all is to be national writers, bearing witness to the intelligence and sensitivity of a specific people. Ours claim to be synthesizing the cultural traditions of the West and African culture. This explains why it is French, English or something else in its expression, being far more concerned with the tastes of a European public which the writer can determine far more precisely and in which he shares without any great difficulty because of his upbringing. There is no need to insist on this situation which is not the sole paradox inherited from colonization and which remains responsible for African writing gravitating around two poles of attraction. One can imagine the mental tightrope that our writers are condemned to master in order to conciliate such paradoxical elements

which are quite alien to one another at best. It is this effort, praiseworthy
as far as the energy needed is concerned, but vain as we see from the very
mediocre results, which gives our literature its hybrid character and the
stamp of cultural interbreeding.

What is to be deplored is that the African element in this culture coming
to birth may well be appallingly reduced in scope. The colonial situation,
the Western education of the writers, the extent and depth of receptivity of
a European public, the language the writer has in common with his public,
all determined the orientation of this writing.

Some of the papers read at the Paris and Rome Congresses were genuine
briefs in favour of this orientation and are quite clear on this point. The
situation could obviously not have been otherwise. The option the writer
took with regard to the political struggle necessarily determined the nature
and objectives of African literature. The writer chose to take an active part
in the fight against colonialism, challenging the world to deny the political
and cultural maturity of Africa. Action had to be taken on two different
fronts. The first step was to convince the West of the divorce existing
between the ideals it professed and the outrage to man's dignity that was
colonialism. Secondly, the great mass of the African people had to be given
hope, first through eliminating the theory of assimilation by producing
proof of the specific nature of Negro culture and traditions and showing
that Africans can be proud of these, as of their history and cultural past.
They also had to be made aware of their inalienable right to freedom. The
objective aimed at was to make Africans realize what was their genuine
personality and arm them so that they could win back their dignity. The
African writer, without any real means of communicating with his people
whose language he does not even know, and from whom he has been cut off
for some decades, had to direct his action mainly towards the West which
he had to convince of the necessity of adopting an attitude towards Africa
which would be more compatible with its democratic ideals. The choice
was not the painful one some have described it as being. Our writers feel
far more at home in Europe than amongst us here. The former has given
them a language whose 'nobility' is a byword; it has given them convenient
concepts and means of apprehending African reality and of interpreting it
in a light which is, to say the least, European. Because of its literary
experience (more than a thousand years of it) it is not unaware of the fact
that literature conceived and defined in this way can make up only a very
weak African version of what really are French or English types of literature.

The European public African writers turn to is homogeneous, sensitive
and one which has long enjoyed well-established traditions. It would weigh
heavily on the fate of a work if a kind of regret for not having given sufficient

attention to the real Africa, in spite of several centuries of contact, did not incline it to welcome any and every new work, so long as it is African. The influence of this public comes not only from its size but also from the ease with which the writer can go towards meeting and communicating with it. Its action is twofold, and affects both the writer and the African public which, necessarily remains subordinate to it, paradoxical though this is. The writer is influenced first of all since he recognizes that Europeans must be firstly catered for, as they judge according to standards to which he cannot give full and entire support in most cases; a kind of tacit complicity welds them to one another. Very often, in fact, the writer forgets that, in borrowing a language and a setting, he is forced to comply with the very structure of these elements, and that in literature neither the language nor the setting constitute tools as they stand, but have specific requirements. The translator is only too well aware of all this: it is a problem he comes up against every day. The writer necessarily has the same headache, try as he does to picture and interpret African reality in a European tongue, a reality which, because no one knew much about it, was considered for a very long time to be primitive and barbarous. Such considerations naturally make the writer eager to insert elements into his work which will flatter the taste of a European public. One of the important reasons for this comes from a certain form of literary profiteering. The European public does not adopt a work because of its taste and language ties, but because it has an enormous advertising apparatus at its disposal. The writer wants to earn his living from his writing and we can hardly blame him for this. Africans, generally speaking, do not read, or read very little. The Dakar symposium made us aware of this. The African writer is not prepared to have his hands tied because of an initial choice; he wants to give a faithful picture of his people whom he swore to liberate, but he does not hesitate to serve this up to Europeans in order to increase his income.

This situation explains why the work is worth something only in so far as it goes ahead of the aspirations of this public which is concerned above all with satisfying its keen appetite for the exotic. Sainville, in answering this question, was only too right when he said: 'What they (the Europeans) want without doubt is to find in the relaxation of a book a means of getting away from the grey, depressing nature of an everyday condition made up more of squabbles and cares than of joy. What is needed to impress them are "isles of beauty", wild, mysterious continents with a strong tinge of the unknown, the extraordinary. In a word, the exotic. Such excessive receptivity, as we know, has already given rise to fake images, purely imaginary pictures and general mystification.'

Consciously or otherwise, and to varying degrees, most of our novelists have been repeating the modern version of the 'noble savage' theme. This taste for the exotic blended with the desire of the writer to be the spokesman of his people explains the vogue for the autobiographic novel and is enough to legitimize the enormous lassitude this 'genre' has created. Some retain only the positive contribution of this public to African literature, while ignoring its enormous responsibility where the present crisis is concerned. A recapitulation of its major themes shows this quite clearly as they are centred on problems which are without any real grip on our people. There is, first of all, the theme of love – one which crosses all racial barriers and is particularly apt to excite the curiosity of Europeans inadequately informed about Africa. Mixed marriages concern only a tiny minority and although they create certain difficulties, they no longer surprise Africans and have ceased to be of any great interest unless they are connected with more important problems.

As to exoticism, nothing too bad can be said about it. A good illustration is the story of the London editor who sent a manuscript back to its African author with the remark 'An excellent novel but not African enough!' Exoticism aims at presenting *homo africanus*, his way of life, in an African Garden of Eden upset by European invaders. All such themes delight Europeans freshly converted to Africanism, as does the subject of cultural cross-breeding and the various inter-civilization contacts. A certain shrillness in the way these are presented falsifies the whole picture although their topical interest is certain. There is nothing more poignant than the painful insecurity of the African intellectual weighing up the value of what he is prepared to abandon, and yet ignorant that what he is adopting will not lead to a certain form of cultural emasculation. He finds himself between two worlds, one overpowering him while the other refuses to die! A theme very close to the 'angst' rife in Europe as a result of the upheaval of the war. In African literature the European public will find certain themes which echo such preoccupations and another wearying theme is that of the colonial situation and the depiction of European life in the colonies as a closed society. In drawing such a picture, the novelist's work is a mere mirror in which the European can observe the problem he is asked to meditate upon and naturally, in most cases, the African exists only as part of the setting. To say he is not 'concerned' would be to go too far; he is concerned, but indirectly. There are few themes in African writing which do not reflect its European trend, the reason for this being the conditions of its coming into being and its development, such conditions having changed to only a very small extent. During the colonial period the writer could not hope for support and encouragement from anyone other than Europeans. The connections which existed then exist today. In the past there was the need to have talks with the colonizers and to show Negroes in a light that he felt to be an honest one. Today, with utterly different conditions of political and cultural promotion, it is amazing to see that our writers are prepared to stay in the old rut.

The problem would be less important if the African public were not reduced to a state of strict subordination because of such attitudes and deprived of all autonomy, as European tastes are forced on it as surely as on the writer. The proof lies in the many awards honouring the talent of a writer which seem to signify with no mean arrogance that certain European criteria have been reached and certain requirements fulfilled which have nothing to do with depicting Africans and their way of life. Although these awards may be given in all equity, they place the African before a *fait accompli*: Europe has given its verdict; the former has only to accept it. Such a situation puts great psychological pressure on the writer. The situation would be quite different if such awards went only to works the public enjoyed, but what happens is that they go to admirable literary monuments quite outside the scope of the public who are content to gaze at them from afar as if they were some magic carpets in another sphere. We must not exaggerate, however. The African learned from the French not to measure the talent of a writer according to the weight of the awards encumbering his masterpiece, but he is disarmed by the power of some critics whose remarks show their poor opinion of African authenticity. There is nothing surprising in the small number of works that won awards because of their strong dose of Africanity or for the favour shown to them by Africans. A critic may recognize a good novel and know nothing about Africa and is often all too ready to reduce the work to a theme he considers essential. European criticism has plenty of leeway owing to the fact that between the African public and itself there is no established African opinion to intervene with the same persuasion. Its sympathy towards Africa in general and towards our literature in particular is undeniable. Its good intentions are those which pave the way to the worst hells for, finally, such criticism leads to imposing its views or to the total falsification of the meaning of a work. This criticism inspires more and more suspicion and ought to pay more attention to such recommendations as those of Lilyan Kesteloot which call on it to 'be less sure of itself, its philosophical ideas and its instinctive reactions, of harking after the picturesque and its humanitarian ambitions'.

What can we say about its highly dogmatic nature, so skilled at disheartening Africans and keeping them outside literary life? There are two basic reasons for its verbosity. The first is the desire to maintain close relations between literature and the human sciences, all these disciplines having as their aim the elucidation of man, of the Negro in particular, according to different perspectives and with different means. But what need is there to harness literature to the chariot of sociology or ethnology, to reduce it to the state of an annexe? This identity of the objectives of these disciplines, and their common interest where Africa is concerned, would seem to explain the ostentation with which European criticism has recourse to a specific language which ends up by only widening the gap which separates the African writer from his real public. The second explanation must be sought for among the African writers who were the first to adopt such an attitude. It is only reasonable that to works which are over-scientific should correspond an erudite type of criticism which strains to link our cultural life closely with that of Europe. That African writers and poets, in particular, should have recourse to the most hermetic type of language to express the plenitude of their thoughts and sensations and that they consider all aesthetic pleasure must be worked for if it is to be enjoyed, is nothing new. What they do not realize, however, is that the African public is leaving them to their complicated games and that they are gesturing to an empty theatre.

In recent years, English-speaking African writers have multiplied the occasions to come together and consider their art, on the conditions needed for its development and on its real scope. The debates held during the conferences at Fourah Bay and Makerere are highly significant. Writers were unanimous in rejecting the claims of such criticism. Ezekiel Mphahlele showed no mean wit in laughing at those who use words as a mouthwash and other coiners of worthless phrases. Even if the thoughts behind some of the words correspond to profound reality, we cannot help wondering what public such critics have in mind or envying English speakers their openness. Such criticism only makes a work more obscure than it may already be and stops the reader from understanding what might have seemed clear and obvious. European critics (and Africans after them) do not try to analyse works; they only want to confirm preconceived ideas. All our poetry is considered only in the light of negritude, in spite of renewed protests made by the vast majority of English-speaking writers who maintain that this concept covers no tangible reality. That some poets place their work under the sign of negritude may be due to their desire to translate the specific and interdependent nature of the Negro race, but that European critics should be only too ready to connect with this concept all manifestations of culture by Negroes is to be deplored as over-simplification. To remedy such aberrations was the aim of the writers who met at Fourah Bay where they express their wish for the University to undertake the elucidation and interpretation of texts: to combat dogmatism in fact! It is obvious that the University is what is best qualified to make an appreciable contribution to the formation of autonomous African criticism which, without turning its back on the outside world, can encourage all signs of original taste and talent. It can, thanks to the means at its disposal

and the possibility it has of not going beyond the bounds of strict objectivity, speed up the consolidation of a school of criticism which will serve
the African public by preparing it first of all so that the latter can draw the
greatest profit from it and, secondly, be an interpreter of this public's
taste which, when analysed, would help the author to know where he
stands in relation to his readers. As those taking part in the conference
agreed, the time when criticism was there to insert an opaque screen
between the work and the public is now over and must give way to another
type of criticism which must be in the line of a genuinely African cultural
development. To attain such a change, more cultural reviews and literary
awards are needed for it is Africans who, eventually, must give their
opinion on the works which, everyone agrees, are written with them in
mind. It is not too much to ask that the fortunes of an African work and the
name of an African writer be subject to the appreciation of an African
public.

The same applies in other countries. That we should even be expressing
such a need proves the influence of European criticism over the arts in
Africa. There is no doubt that the joint pressure of criticism and a European public give a quite special look to African literature, determining the
form and meaningful nature of the writing, exerting a dual and somewhat
contradictory influence on the writer, expecting from the work a certain
dépaysement and opening up new worlds, but there is no renunciation of the
comfort of these certainties. The writer is thus forced to keep the customer
in mind and to give his goods a special finish for the foreign market. This is
all the easier in that a certain compatibility exists (which may be fatal to
African literature) between the ravenous appetite of Europeans for everything exotic and the option the African writer has taken for realism and
depicting the way of life of his country. In most cases, this kind of work
(novels mainly) loses any literary quality it might have had, since the form
is quite scandalously sacrificed to ideas, the writer being concerned only
with satisfying his public's thirst and making the most of the occasion to
get his message across. No further proof is needed of the danger of such a
situation. Often, the book is no longer a relation between form and meaning
in the way Gaeton Picon had in mind, but becomes a mere sign. Europeans
are satisfied with this and, unconcerned by the problem, are prepared to
show great gentleness towards our writers, welcoming whatever comes in
the guise of negritude and, because of their lack of discrimination,
encourage mediocrity.

Critics would do well to consider the example of Pierre-Henri Simon, an
example more conducive to the betterment of our literature. Too experienced and shrewd a critic to be misled by the clamour of incurable pane-
gyrists, he said about *L'Aventure Ambiguë* that it was 'at times too dogmatic

and overwritten with everybody, even "la grande Royale", talking like philosophers. The book is touching in the thought that has gone into its making and in the lofty tone in which this is expressed.' This appreciation is useful to the author starting out, since it enables him to become aware of his weak points and eliminate them. It is perhaps because our literature is still so very young that European critics treat it differently, but there is no better method than excessive indulgence for condemning it to tardy youth. Sartre made no mistake about this when he remarked on certain dangers inherent in leniency towards African writing. The author of *Black Orpheus*, condemning the attitude of critics, said 'This delighted indulgence (is the kind) parents show towards their children on their birthday'. He puts the public on their guard against paternalism and assimilation tendencies and calls on it not to reduce literary creations to a mere 'homage rendered to French culture'.

There is no doubt that attempts at assimilation have been hanging fire. For a long time there was a strong trend towards trying to integrate our writers into European literary movements, whilst others wanted to fit them into the ranks of followers of whatever literary master was in vogue at the time. The former fought hard against all this which could only widen the gap separating them from their real public. Senghor, one of the very few African writers capable of amazing creative powers allied to a no less fertile gift of meditating on his art, rejected these claims: 'If they want to find masters for us', he riposted in *Négritude et Humanisme*, 'it would be more apt to look for them in Africa.' This attitude is the only good one. Africa, in her profound wisdom, will always prefer to go to the master rather than to the disciple.

It would not be right to say all European criticism comes under the same flag but the fact remains that it does not always give budding African literature the help it has the right to expect. The only attitude this criticism could take which would help in promoting our writing would be in maintaining a stronger conviction that the future of our writing will become concrete in the continent itself. African literature, expressed in any form whatever, cannot, for innumerable reasons, be considered as the common property of Europe and Africa but must be appreciated for itself as an element of cultural solidarity. This has not always been the case and a study of relations between our writing and the European public and critics, leads one to conclude that these relations, implying total subordination, are obviously not of a nature to reinforce links between the writer and his African public.

It is remarkable that this should be so. When we look at the situation of our literature in Africa itself, we see that the public, thanks to the effect of European criticism and the writer's own attitude, is condemned to an appalling passivity, its role being limited to ingurgitating works other people accepted in place of it. It is as if Africans had no literary traditions or were incapable of any enthusiasm for things of the mind. Not being consulted in the matter, they cannot be the 'judge and censor' they ought to be. If there was a policy to have such literature without Africans at all, no better method could be found.

In actual fact, our writing is like Soviet industry before Khrushchev, concerned only with production, the consumer being forced to do everything else. You must agree the situation of African writers is rather special in that they want to be representatives of a people whose aspirations they do not always worry about. It is easy to take refuge behind the problems of language barriers and the very small number of those capable of having access to the works produced. Such things are undoubtedly important but what really matters is that all works, thanks to translations, are sent out all over Africa. The public is large enough to enable one to tackle the financial implications. Readers show remarkable sensitivity in Nigeria and the Cameroons, have excellent means of information and cultural exchanges at their disposal and make the most of a healthy policy for the encouragement of vocations in the young and the protection of their cultural heritage.

Senegal which, very rightly, is considered the homeland of African arts, has made enormous sacrifices in organizing the Festival of Negro Arts but, to say the least, it does not enjoy the literary life it deserves. Senegalese critics seem determined to try to satisfy everybody; this results in the exasperating conformity which, in the long run, will make our school of criticism a mere bureau for exchanging useful methods. Conditions in English-speaking countries are quite different and we ought to pay more attention to their progressive literary experiments from our side of the language border. In Senegal, as in the majority of French-speaking countries, there is not one cultural review, everyone having recourse to the excellent *Présence Africaine*. The former countries are showing fresh initiative every day. The list is a long one, going from *Black Orpheus* in Nigeria, *Transition* in Uganda to *Contrast* in South Africa. It is not important that a lot of these should have only an ephemeral existence, so long as the experience is renewed and carried on by others and contact is maintained between the writer and the African public. In French-speaking Africa there is only *Abbia*, an excellent Cameroonian review which has succeeded in winning a vast audience in a very short time. This success is proof of the crying need that Africans and others had of it.

It is true that, where information is concerned, the problem of language inevitably crops up but the number of Africans able to easily understand books is increasing regularly. The impressive education programmes being put into action in the various States makes it possible to see the future in a more hopeful light. In ten years' time, the African public will be five times as large as it is now. For Senegal alone (a significant index) the number of educational establishments preparing pupils for the *baccalauréat* has increased from six to fourteen since independence. It goes without saying that for a long time yet a large part of our population will have to remain outside any intellectual life because of the existing language problems, although there is every reason for believing that illiteracy is everywhere on the decrease.

The author has to think of the future when he is writing and it is not conceivable that he should leave his African public aside for mere personal gain. It is of course obvious that in order to appreciate any piece of writing, the standard of rentability is not the only one to be considered. Those taking part in the conferences held at the Universities of Dakar and Fourah Bay insisted on the need for more time being given to the study of African literature in our Universities. This teaching could then be extended to all levels of education and in this way our writers would play an important part in the formation of a sensitive, receptive public. The moment has come at last when it is necessary to create works which are genuinely African in scope, form and orientation and not anything second-rate which a long look would quickly show to be without any real substance. Not only is it high time to question the strictly literary value of certain works, but to regret that in certain circumstances our novelists do not choose to write an essay or a treatise. Art has nothing to lose in remaining 'a language of forms', according to the definition of Gaeton Picon. The present state of African literature can only make us worried when we see that, alongside such 'giants' as Senghor, Birago Diop, Oyono and others, we have to put writers who, although highly prolific, show a contempt for form which is quite amazing. Next, there is 'the extreme youth of our literature and the need to let time do its work, separating the wheat from the chaff'. These arguments, often adopted by partisans of that excessive indulgence enjoyed by our writers, do not deserve any consideration. We are a young and impatient people and literature which can boast of the names quoted above is ripe for great things: only the conditions needed for its full development and the hatching out of fresh talent remain to be realized. Whether what we are going through can be called 'growing pains' or a 'period of adaptation' is of little importance as this phase is essential if progress is to be made. The principles which inspired this inevitable change had to give place to more literary considerations. The exotic note is bound to die away some time or other and the European public will soon be saturated by a certain kind of writing. The survival of our literature can only be assured if it accepts being the reflection of a special type of sensitivity, the echo of African aspiration and is addressed to a public that is primarily African.

This has been well understood in Nigeria and the Cameroons where interesting experiments are being carried out which give a new and intensely African look to the latest works. It is comforting to note that the latter can be proud of a school of young poets who combine their activity with their work in the Administration and are engaged in their first campaign; men whom Senghor described as being 'nourished with the suck of the earth' and who have never set foot in a university. True poetry is not necessarily concerned with academic language and we can only feel pleased that our Western inheritance has been unable to wipe out our African patrimony.

At the Kampala Conference, English-speaking writers gave an account of the exclusively European trend in our literature and explained such a trend as inevitable since the majority of writers did their studies in Europe where they discovered their vocation, while others who had a university on their doorstep were able to remain in close contact with their people. An objective study of African works written in French and in English shows that those writing in English are more alive to African reality. This is seen in the extraordinary vitality of Nigerian literature, whereas ours is still marking time. Our English-speaking neighbours, who are not to be taken for the only models acceptable, understood how necessary it was for the writer to get a large following in Africa itself and to remain in close communion with his people. Two solutions are open to him: either to raise the public to his own level or to go more than half-way to meet its tastes. The first solution, given the present situation, is out of the question; the second, as experience has shown, must be adopted within the framework of a real cultural promotion. Only one method is possible to remedy the existing state of things: namely, a closer connection with traditional culture. To expect the public to depersonalize itself and give up its sensibility in order to be worthy of a certain kind of literature is obviously too much to ask. The wise course is to use the usual methods of intellectual advance and aesthetic enjoyment, however new the message destined for this public may seem.

Such a slant would help our situation very much and the writer and his public would no longer be at odds. The public's lack of attention to works written in a language not their own is striking and their enthusiasm and fondness for inspiring creations are famous. The often second-rate programmes put out by Radio Senegal are more popular (because of a certain social realism no doubt) than works of real literary value. Given the people's appreciation of problems which really are part of their daily lives, one can understand how crude technique is so willingly passed over as long as the programmes entertain. What greater proof could one have of our people's capacity for enthusiasm than the reception given to certain songs that are poetic and full of feeling? They need only be broadcast once to be on everyone's lips the next day. There is, for instance, a particularly beautiful song, evocative of the famous Taj Mahal in which the composer tries to console himself over the death of his wife. There is nothing surprising in the fact that the people should enjoy such poetry, given their own tales, enigmas, proverbs and sacred hymns. There is often an inclination to turn away from such literature merely through our own ignorance of its true nature. This is the heart of the matter. Given the weak echo that a given work raised in home territory, people were quick to speak of imposture. The situation is, to say the least, an uncomfortable one. The writer speaks in the name of a people who never elected him and which he does not consider an authority in the matter. Being able to obtain an outside hearing, he becomes a link connecting our continent with the rest of the world and claims to fight for the triumphing of values and the acceptance of what is genuine in our culture. He tries to show the world that we are neither without a past nor a culture which owe nothing to Europe and which concede nothing to others. This is a long business and, unlike the struggle against colonialism, will hardly leave him stranded without any real objectives. Even if the authenticity of African cultures were to be realized by the rest of the world, it would naturally be the work of our writers and intellectuals to interpret them. The greater evil would undoubtedly be to travesty them rather than deny them all originality.

The role of the writer must never be depreciated. That he should be without real contact with his public is due to the fact that the mission he has been entrusted with has not been fulfilled as well as it might be. There is no end to his good intentions or to the awareness of his duty. He sings of the wealth and soul of our culture and praises the hundred qualities in it but is careful not to delve into tradition and illustrate such treasures. He leaves us with the disagreeable impression of being a preacher unconvinced himself, a skilful handler of myths. Experience shows us, however, that those writers known to Africans and esteemed by them are the ones who realize their work will be worth something only if it is rooted in a traditional literature in which the writer, even though he may know it perfectly well, at times feels ill at ease. He has to make a considerable effort to adapt himself since in many major ways it is different from what he is used to. Western literature cultivates selfish enjoyment and, whatever people say, is written with a privileged minority in mind. The reader can enter such a world if he is apart from the group and inward-looking, just like a theatre public which needs the complicity of the dark to make its enjoyment absolute. Western literature speaks a special language to each member of the public and does not suffer any difference in interpretation. This is quite unlike traditional literature which is the whole group's common property, or, rather, can only be conceived of as an element binding the group together. Such common property cannot possibly be monopolized by a minority: neither the tales, enigmas nor sacred hymns can take on all their importance unless those listening to them are in close communion with one another. Man himself is of no value except in so far as he occupies his real place in the community and in the universe.

Another element which makes for disjunction in the expression of a writer who has not been to a traditional African school, is that our literature avoids anything that will exalt the individual who remains in harmonious union with the group: neither selfishness nor self-centredness are conceivable. The theme of loneliness is unknown; only a common fate prevails. Our literature is functional, not because it rejects aesthetic intentions but because it does not separate aesthetic pleasure from the rest. What it wants to do is to be at the service of man and thus is engaged in life. This particularity ought to be a factor in bringing the African writer back to his origins but, more often than not, this leads to engagement and not participation. There is a basic divorce at this point. The notion of engagement, as inherited from the West, is almost always fatal to the work which remains within the dimensions of a stroke of luck. The form of engagement, moreover, is to a certain extent a cause for division because the work only represents a tendency or a group. Engagement in the traditional literature is total, with the whole community taking part, and treating it as part of life in all its aspects. An initiation, this literature constitutes a mine of information, a repertory of precepts and crystal-clear evidence of what is permanent in African values. Its only aim is to contribute to the enrichment of man and to insert him into his milieu. It is the expression of the wisdom and sense of beauty shown by the group and remains, with art, the best means of handing on its experience of life. Its main objective is to help man find his real place in the world and not further any kind of minority entertainment. Such an attribute governs its whole attitude towards life and reality.

One might reach the overhasty conclusion, after considering the oral nature and fixed character of certain genres such as proverbs and sacred songs, that there is a certain unawareness of development in certain spheres. It would be easy to show that this literature is concerned only with the past and that the experience of the ancestors touches on the present. It is also true to say it remains concerned with the present. The very newness of our writing in European languages and its individual character make it impossible to extend the parallel in certain directions but we can attribute to traditional literature, in its most vital forms, a constant effort to capture reality and to actualize it, even if this means a certain didacticism.

The functional character of this literature determines its form more than its oral nature. People have exaggerated the need to make material easy to memorize and reproduce. In fact, where certain genres are concerned, only the themes and teaching of the Ancients are given. The storyteller always has to enliven the tale his public knows by heart. It is because of the need to draw on life that the work is necessarily orientated towards the actual. Art shares this tendency with literature and both are closely linked to a special type of society whose attitude towards life and beauty it is their task to interpret. It is by no means pure chance that most of the masks are made of perishable material, the word dying as soon as its mission has been accomplished. Our art and literature die with the society which gives them their *raison d'etre*, to be born again in other forms in order to express with greater fluidity the harmony and balance that exist in man's relations with his universe. It is in this attitude towards life that we find the final element which illustrates so perfectly the stand taken by most African writers who, in spite of their declarations in favour of Negro cultures, see to it that they do not draw their inspiration from them. In the West, art and literature are a means of protesting against reality. Camus, in *l'Homme Révolté*, gives us a dazzlingly clear illustration of the ambiguity inherent in the situation of the artist, in his rebellion against reality and his attempts to put his world together again in a mosaic of coherence and intelligibility. Baudelaire before him, and Malraux, said no less. The latter understands art as being against destiny. Our art and literature, in spite of a certain similarity in creative methods and processes, shows not revolt but equilibrium. One can now see that the divorce between the African writer and his public is more serious than has been thought up to now.

It would be illusory to think that a novel needs only to be set in Africa for it to be acceptable to the public. Experience has shown that the latter favour works that are rooted deeply in cultural traditions and that nothing has equalled the enthusiasm reserved for the works of Birago Diop and Bernard Dadié. No one has participated more fervently than our story-tellers in the attempt to restore dignity to the African. It is true that no trace is to be found in their work of that vehemence and ostentatious attitude which were characteristic of our literature before independence and yet it is they alone who have given proof of the cultural maturity of Africa while safeguarding the original purity of her literature. Only they have understood that the African writer can make the most of his virtual-ities only if he is in contact with the earth that gave him suck. We can only attribute the succes of a Diop, a Dadié or the Nigerian Achebe to the desire to delve deep down into tradition and there is nothing surprising in the parallels to be found in their writings. Similar experiences are expressed with equal skill and artistry and there is the same effort to express what is most genuine in the depths of the African soul through the strictest respect for European languages. Nowhere else does one so powerfully feel the need to be heard by an African public.

Another example of the stimulus such an orientation can have is the situation of the African theatre working in French which is now at a dead standstill, and the Nigerian theatre which shows tremendous invention and vigour. The former is excessively concerned with style, attempts to satisfy the aesthetic sense of the public and has no influence on the general mass of the people; the latter, in spite of the risks implicit in such methods, draws its inspiration from reality and has close links with the public. That our literature must be blended with tradition does not imply encouraging chauvinism or going back to primitivity. Colonialism marked the African indelibly and no will in the world can eliminate the consequences of the encounter between Africa and the West. Our literature and art, in their modern forms, cannot but be the result of lines of force which have their source in Africa as much as in Europe. What is surprising is the desire to create an African literature ignorant of everything African and to show the cultural maturity of Africa without having any care for her most original creations which are the greatest proof of her wisdom, profound insight into the soul of man and deep sense of beauty.

The trouble is that we have been summoned to a meeting with the universal too early and it is characteristic of our times to be impatient and to insist that every man must be ready to cope with this meeting. We must of course see in this invitation the implicit recognition of the value of our cultures but must not lose sight of the need at this first stage not only to consolidate the authenticity of our culture and literature, but to act in such a way that our spokesmen absorb this fully from the outset.

The Society of African Culture, in its fine letter to African Catholics participating in the Oecumenical Council, recalled the fact that 'we must no longer be content to receive: the time has come for us to give'. It is obvious that we can offer nothing more acceptable at this meeting with the universal than the richness of our culture and the permanence of our values. There is therefore no need for us to abandon our true personality. Senghor, with the accents of Montaigne, has declared that 'in the face of every people you will find the different features of the human condition'.

Our literature will only get its health back when writers are convinced that it is in Africa herself that they must look for these features of the 'human condition' – with the means Europe has inevitably endowed them with and whose effectiveness cannot be questioned. All have had occasion to state and reiterate the pride they have taken in the wealth of African culture. It is high time this feeling was expressed in some concrete way so that the writer, in going back to the sources, may become reconciled with his public. Such a reform – the only way liable to assure the continuity of our literature – will have to be undertaken by our writers themselves. They must be as convinced as the Haitian, Jacques Stephen Alexis, that 'a great work is born from the dialectical conjunction of individual talent and the collective genius of the people'.

It is the task of the writers to work for the creation of a literature which, backed by African cultural tradition, will appeal before all else to the intelligence and sensitivity of Africans: a literature whose value will only be recognized throughout the world if it is truly representative of the aspirations and aesthetic expression of the people.

Ali A. Mazrui

▼▼▼▼▼▼▼▼▼▼▼▼▼▼▼▼▼▼▼▼▼▼▼▼▼▼▼▼▼▼▼▼▼

The Patriot as an Artist[1]

[1966]

THE relationship between patriotism and literature in East Africa
has three broad dimensions. The first dimension concerns the very
act of writing itself. In a society where written creative literature is a
relative novelty, and where this activity is invested with cultural prestige in
response to the Western impact, the fact that people write at all becomes an
act of national rejuvenation.

The second dimension of relationship between literature and patriotism in
East Africa concerns the themes of the literature itself. In this case it is not
merely the writing that is an expression of nationalism, but what is written.

The third dimension in this interplay between national sentiment and
literary expression concerns the kind of links which should be forged
between African literature and the literary heritage of the outside world.
Within this general area lies the place of translation and of languages
generally in relation to cultural nationalism.

Let us take each of these broad areas of discourse in turn.

THE PEN AND THE PATRIOT

National assertion is sometimes a response to prior national humiliation.
The form which nationalism takes is intimately related in such instances
with the kind of humiliation to which the nation was previously subjected.
Among the factors which contributed to the relegation of the African to a
back seat on the cultural train of human history was the absence of writing
in the life-style of many African societies. Sir Phillip Mitchell, who served
as Governor of both Kenya and Uganda, expressed a typical external sentiment when he marvelled once at Africa's isolation from the rest of the
world before Western imperialism tore off the curtains of mystery. Sir

---

[1] For our purposes in this paper we need not sharply distinguish between
patriotism and nationalism. But one way of distinguishing the two is to regard
nationalism as a more defensive and less secure form of patriotism. Nationalism
might then be classified as a special kind of patriotism.

Phillip was particularly surprised that any people, particularly 'a people wide open to the sea' as East Africans were, should have reached the twentieth century without an alphabet of their own.

Statements of this kind abound in the literature of imperial assessments of the African. For an individual to be illiterate was something which at the time was pretty common in Western countries themselves; but for a society to be without the means of written expression was supposed to be the ultimate signal of cultural retardation. Indians and Arabs, and others elsewhere in the Orient, had also been colonial subjects; but these were assigned higher places in the gradation of human types partly because they had been capable of committing their thoughts to writing independently of Western influence. But the case of the African and his primeval lack of literacy was seen as different.

The absence of the written word affected other areas of evaluating the place of the African in world civilization. Among these must be included the simple point of whether the African had a history at all. This doubt goes far back in the story of Western assessments of the African. One distinguished exponent of this scepticism in the modern period is the current Regius Professor of Modern History at Oxford, Professor Hugh Trevor-Roper. In 1963 Trevor-Roper said in a television broadcast in Britain: 'Perhaps in the future there will be some African history to teach. But at present there is none; there is only the history of Europeans in Africa. The rest is darkness . . . and darkness is not a subject of history.'[2]

This kind of interpretation is usually founded on a conception of history which is perhaps excessively literary. It thinks of historical evidence as being basically written documentary evidence. A people that is therefore without an adequate body of written evidence and records of past lives falls under the shadow of historical scepticism. It continues to be relatively easy for many commentators from more literate societies to regard African peoples South of the Sahara as being in the main peoples without a historical personality.

Nationalists like Kwame Nkrumah have sometimes tried to cope with this criticism by demonstrating the availability of a large body of written records, many of them in Arabic, on which the history of West Africa might be founded. And yet this line of counter-argument is itself a concession to the Trevor-Ropers. It is an admission that to prove a historical personality one needs written records. Not all African societies in the different corners of the continent could indeed meet even the standards assumed by the

---

[2] See *The Listener*, November 28, 1963. This point is also discussed in my Inaugural Lecture at Makerere, *Ancient Greece in African Political Thought* (Nairobi: E. A. Publishing House, 1967) pp. 22–5.

retorts of African nationalists like Nkrumah.[3] Finally, there is the place of the written word in creative literature itself. Students of African cultures have lately allowed a place of respectability to oral literature – the songs, hymns and morality stories which have formed a part of African traditional life. And yet creative literature of the written kind was invested by the entire educational system in the Colonies with aesthetic prestige. Classics of English literature or French literature were part of high culture itself. Even in English-speaking Africa, relatively less flamboyant in its utilization of cultural borrowings from the metropolitan imperial power, quotations from Shakespeare or Tennyson or Wordsworth became part of the oratorical techniques of politicians, as well as of literary people.[4]

The absence of written creative literature from the life-style of many African societies helped to aggravate a sense of cultural inadequacy among Africans during the Colonial period. If then, the absence of the written word was intimately a part of Africa's sense of humiliation during the Colonial period, the outburst of written creativity among Africans since those early days did in turn become an intimate part of Africa's vindication of herself. That Africans could write novels or plays or even operas was in the initial stages acclaimed by Africans themselves as a phenomenon of cultural vindication. African writers have sometimes assumed heroic dimensions not simply because of their literary skills but because they were playing a part in firmly placing the African on the map of global literary civilization.

In East Africa the first book-length literary achievement of political significance was not a work of the imagination as such. It was Jomo Kenyatta's *Facing Mount Kenya*, a personalized anthropological study. There is no doubt that Kenyatta's stature in East Africa in those early days was significantly enhanced by the simple fact that he had succeeded in becoming an author. A sophisticated book in the English language to his credit constituted part of his credentials for political leadership at large.

Much later a fellow Kikuyu, James Ngugi, burst into prominence by being the first indigenous East African novelist. Again, this was not simply a case of eulogizing an author for his success strictly as an author. It was also a case of eulogizing a cultural pioneer who was opening up new areas of national vindication for his people. He was demonstrating an East African capacity to join the flow of creative fiction.

[3] See his address to the First International Congress of Africanists. *Proceedings of the First International Congress of Africanists*, edited by Lalage Bown and Michael Crowder (London: Longmans, 1964) p. 8.

[4] The role of English literature in political rhetoric in Africa is discussed more fully in my paper 'Some Socio-political functions of English literature in Africa', presented at a Conference on 'Language Problems in Developing Nations', Centre for Applied Linguistics, Washington D.C.

More recently, there has been Solomon Mbabi-Katana's short operatic exercise *The Marriage of Nyakato*. Again, the significance of the work lies almost exclusively in its pioneering status. It is too brief and simple to be regarded as a major achievement, but it is a venture into a new cultural area for Africa.

The uncritical acclamation of literary pioneering poses its own problems. Just as Africans have sometimes acclaimed each other's writings as an expression of national vindication, so have foreign critics sometimes acclaimed African writing as an assertion of their own liberalism. Dubious literary exercises by Africans have sometimes met with Western enthusiasm mainly because the exercises were from Africa. In this kind of situation, some Africans themselves have reacted against the acclaim of the outside world. Amos Tutuola's *The Palm-Wine Drinkard* was widely applauded abroad as a great achievement in creative fantasy and unusual diction. Yet, many African critics regarded the external applause as an attempt to patronize naïve attempts by an under-educated African. Since then, there has been widespread African criticism of publishers who, in the words of Lewis Nkosi, 'are in such indecent haste to put into print any mediocre talent from Africa'.

What all this means is that the same nationalism which is capable of acclaiming mediocre African works simply because they are African finds itself deeply offended if the works are acclaimed by Westerners for the same reason. There is a conviction that indulgence by the foreigner is a form of indignity for the native. What is not good enough by the canons of European writers when judging each other ought not to be permitted to be good enough when judging the performance of an African writer.

Within East Africa there has also been discussion on whether the region has been a literary desert. *East Africa Journal*, among other publications in East Africa, has carried within its pages vigorous self-evaluation by East Africans on 'the barrenness' of the area in literary work. There have also been seminars and conferences and discussions on the same theme. On the other hand, particularly since 1967, the defenders of the East African literary scene have come to the fore with the assertion that the region was abounding with innovation and literary fertility. All that it had lacked were sometimes adequate avenues for its expression. Certainly the new journal *Zuka*, issued by Oxford University Press and devoted entirely to creative literature and criticism, bases its right to existence on the argument that the amount of creativity available in East Africa has yet to find adequate outlets. Each of the University Colleges in East Africa has one literary magazine – *Nexus* at Nairobi, *Darlite* at Dar-es-Salaam, and *Penpoint* at Makerere University College in Kampala. It is not clear how many of these ventures will manage to sustain themselves over a period of time. What is clear is that there is in East Africa an outburst of literary activity, of very mixed quality, aided and abetted both by publishers and by academic departments of English within the region. At least one of those academic departments has also worked hard to interest publishers to get under-graduates to write about cultural aspects of their own region, and seeks to encourage graduate students to collect and record as much of the oral literature of East Africa as possible. Some of the publishers have been daring and courageous in the commercial risks they have been willing to take with untried students on unusual projects. Yet their critics would still insist that this is all part of a ruthless commercialism to purvey African goods on the literary market, even if many of them are defective or even rotten.

And yet the balance of argument is not all on one side when we try to assess the desirability of encouraging British publishers to take greater, even if less discriminate interest, in the work of African students. It may indeed be true that a lot of bad stuff may be published. And yet it is worth remembering that all national literatures have grown up within a vigorous relationship of co-existence between the bad and the good. Indeed, that is perhaps how aesthetic discrimination becomes meaningful and standards of selectivity in taste attain sophisticated complexity. To promote a *wealth of literature* in Africa might not be the same thing as promoting *good literature*. The desire to build up a wealth of literature in Africa puts a premium on diversity, even at the apparent cost of qualitative consistency. This desire for diversity also includes in itself a temporal humility – a feeling that what many regard as 'weak' or even 'really bad' in this month and age might conceivably be credited with some literary merit some time in the future. For a geographical region which has yet to build up a literary heritage of the written kind, the correct policy might be the one which Mao's China momentarily supported and then abandoned – 'Let a hundred flowers bloom,' and hope for the best!

BIOGRAPHY AND CULTURE

But it is not merely in the act of abundant writing that East Africa seeks to realize a cultural heritage. It is also in part in the themes which have so far interested East African writers.

Lionel Trilling once discussed Freud's place within literary creativity – and concluded that his place lay in the 'simple proposition that literature is dedicated to the conception of the self'.[5]

Freud's preoccupation with the self at the conscious and the subconscious

[5] See Trilling, *Beyond Culture; Essays on Literature and Learning* (Penguin Books, 1967 Edition), p. 90.

provides a meeting point between psychology and the literary imagination in its attempt to portray selfhood at large.

This point in turn establishes a connection, for example, a lyric and an autobiography. Both modes are an attempt either at self-expression or at portraying an aspect of selfhood.

In discussing literature in East Africa some attention has therefore to be paid to the struggling or nascent art of autobiography. So far much of the autobiographical writing in East Africa in the English language comes from Kenya, and much of that is connected with the Mau Mau insurrection and the place of individual personalities within that insurrection. Of course Jomo Kenyatta's *Facing Mount Kenya* was itself written well before the Mau Mau outbreak. It was also primarily an exercise in social anthropology, seeking to define and explain 'the tribal life of the Gikuyu'. And yet there persistently remained within the book a personal dimension which in places virtually converted the book into an autobiographical exercise. B. Malinowski opened his introduction to Kenyatta's book with the slogan: 'Anthropology begins at home.' He then referred to the two factors which gave the book its deeply personal character. One of these was Mr Kenyatta's own commitment to the pride of the Kikuyu people, and the other was the extent to which he borrowed from the depths of his own experience in order to portray a picture of the lives of his fellow-Kikuyu. 'As a first-hand account of a representative African culture, as an invaluable document in the principles underlying culture-contact and change; last, not least, as a personal statement of the new outlook of a progressive African, this book will rank as a pioneering achievement of outstanding merit.'[6]

And Kenyatta himself presented his credentials in terms like 'I can therefore speak as a representative of my people, with personal experience of many different aspects of their life.'[7]

The nature of his portrayal of the Kikuyu people probably converted Kenyatta, as I have argued elsewhere, into one of the earliest proponents of the philosophy of negritude in Africa. He might not have known of the label of negritude when he was making his contribution to its philosophy, but the whole idea and subject-matter of his book, *Facing Mount Kenya*, rested on some of the basic assumptions of that philosophy. Leopold Senghor defined negritude as:

Negritude is the whole complex of civilized values – cultural, economic, social and political – which characterize the Black Peoples, or more precisely, the Negro African world. All these values are essentially

---

[6] Malinowski's Introduction to *Facing Mount Kenya* (first published 1938) (London: Secker and Warburg, 1959 Edition), pp. vii to xiv.
[7] Preface, *Facing Mount Kenya*, p. xx.

informed by intuitive reason. . . . The sense of communion, the gift of myth making, the gift of rhythm, such are the essential elements of Negritude, which you will find indelibly stamped on all the works and activities of the Black Man.[8]

Yet it is all very well to revel in the ways of traditional Africa. What is often more to the point is to specify those ways in concrete ethnological examples. Kenyatta did attempt to do precisely that in *Facing Mount Kenya*.

And yet African nationalism has been ambivalent about the study of anthropology itself. Writing in a journal of anthropology in 1934, Margery Perham suggested that 'the newly self-conscious African' was quick to suspect the academic mind which called a study of the African 'anthropology' and of the white man 'sociology'. Seemingly vindicating Dame Perham's words nearly thirty years later President Nkrumah suggested to the First Congress of Africanists in Ghana in 1962 that African studies from then on should, in his words, 'change its course from anthropology to sociology'.

But if this is the conflict between anthropology and nationalism, why should Kenyatta's anthropological study be deemed a contribution to the nationalistic concept of negritude? The reason is precisely because the concept of negritude is the meeting point between nationalism and anthropology. Negritude is often an exercise in romantic ethnology. Most African nationalists who share this vision have concentrated on the romance: Kenyatta provided the ethnology as well.

He did indeed combine his description with commitment, his analysis with personal involvement. And as he evaluated the imperial interference with the customary modes of behaviour of the Kikuyu people, Kenyatta was moved to reaffirm that to deny the Kikuyu the right to their traditions was not merely to deny them their personality as Kikuyu – but was to deny them their dignity as human beings. For 'it is the culture which he inherits that gives a man his human dignity'. Perhaps the whole philosophy of negritude in Africa rests on this simple, but fundamental premise.[9]

Kenyatta's book is also literary in the use it makes of some African parables, sometimes connected with wild animals and their presumed ways and organization. Particularly memorable is the Kikuyu story about a pact concluded between an elephant and a man, and the thunderstorm which led to the annexation of the man's tent by the bigger animal he had wished to befriend.[10]

---

[8] See Senghor 'Negritude and African Socialism' *St. Anthony's papers on African Affairs, No. 2*, Edited by Kenneth Kirkwood (Chatto and Windus, 1963), p. 11.
[9] See *Facing Mount Kenya*, pp. 196–7. This point is also discussed in my article 'East Africa in the Stream of African Thought', *Internationale Spectator* (Brussels), 1968, pp. 764–8.
[10] *Facing Mount Kenya*, pp. 47–52.

A more explicitly autobiographical work linked to Kikuyu history is Josiah Kariuki's account of his role and fortunes within the Mau Mau insurrection. This is in his book '*Mau Mau*' *Detainee*. In many ways Kariuki's book compares favourably with that political classic in African autobiographical exercises, Nkrumah's *Ghana, the Autobiography of Kwame Nkrumah*. Kariuki describes the way he finds himself changed by the very account he heard about Kenyatta as a new leader who had come back home from abroad to speak up for the rights of his people. From simple juvenile hero-worship Kariuki drifted into the awesome ceremonies of taking oaths stark-naked, and committing himself in readiness to kill, for the sake of a broader cause.

Another autobiography connected with the Mau Mau Insurrection is that of Waruhiu Itote or the General China of the movement. The man was evidently a key figure in that movement. His own story about the matter has therefore an important dimension of interest, but the particular book he has produced, though fascinating in parts, falls considerably short of literary or historical adequacy. A weightier book is that of Karari Njama and Donald L. Barnett entitled, *Mau Mau from Within*. Barnett is basically an editor-in-chief behind the scenes, trying to put a stamp of social science respectability to the more spontaneous narrative given by one of the participants in the Mau Mau movement. The book does in part succeed in taking us behind the scenes and into the forests, and tells us not only about the relationship between the fighters and the ideas that agitated them, but also between them and those they mixed with – their women, their relatives, their friends all committed *to* their *course*. Njama's account is in many ways intensely personalized, and is often enriched by that very fact. Barnett, who appears as 'co-author', is in fact a kind of explicator, interpreting the broader social implications of each personal sector of the Kikuyu author's own account.

Tom Mboya's own book, *Freedom and After* – acclaimed by the *New York Times* when it came out as one of the books of the year for 1963 is also partly autobiographical and partly a personal testament. In the last decade of Kenya's struggle for independence Mboya was in many ways the towering diplomatic symbol of Kenya's nationalism. He achieved international pre-eminence, and his sheer sophistication and eloquence was often an effective counter to the imperial propaganda on the activism and primitive nature of the Mau Mau Insurrection. Ferhat Abbas, himself a highly sophisticated Algerian, had served in his day as a public leader of the Algerian Government in exile. In his case, too, the polished sophistication of the man was necessary to lend greater diplomatic respectability to the cause of the Algerian rebels on the battlefield. Mboya was to Kenya, in that respect, what Ferhat Abbas was to the Algerian cause. Of course there were important differences between the two situations, and Mboya was never explicitly a spokesman for the Mau Mau rebels. What mattered, however, was that the Mau Mau, perhaps even more than the Algerian insurrection-ists, had a tarnished image of primordial brutishness. The bad image of the Mau Mau could so easily have affected the image of Kenya's national-ism at large and its right to fulfilment. Did Kenya deserve to have the doors of political participation in the modern sense left open? Many liberals abroad wanted reassurance that there was more to Kenya's nationalism than a mere withdrawal into the primordial brutishness. Tom Mboya provided this evidence. His polish, bearing and powers of articulation were, to all intents and purposes, unsurpassed anywhere in English-speaking Africa. In *Freedom and After*, one gets a glimpse of Mboya's own self-conception and of his vision of the tasks in Kenya and how they needed to be handled.

Although many of the biographies have come forth from Kenya, other parts of East Africa have not been unproductive in this area. Of particular note is an account by a revolutionary on one hand and an account by a deposed king on another. The revolutionary is John Okello, the man who is credited with having spearheaded the Zanzibar revolution. He has given his version of what happened in a fascinating book entitled *Revolution in Zanzibar*. As a foil to this book we have a king's story in Sir Edward Mutesa's book *The Desecration of my Kingdom*. It is in this that he tries both to provide a renewed historical vindication for the institutions of Buganda and a statement about those events since independence which culminated in his flight from Uganda to the United Kingdom in 1966. He fled in the wake of the military conquest of his palace by the armed forces of the Central Government of Uganda. At first this seemed like the sort of book which the Central Government of Uganda might have been tempted to ban from the country. What happened, on the contrary, was that it was serialized in the Party newspaper of the governing Uganda People's Congress, *The People*. The Uganda Government, in serializing a major book by its own arch enemy, displayed remarkable astuteness. It undercut the publishers in what was potentially the most important single market for the book, and it let the glaring defects of the book expose themselves within the hospitable pages of a hostile newspaper.

In Okello's book we get in a dramatic form the persistent intermingling of nationalism with racial sentiment in the African continent. The little island of Zanzibar captured the clash between the idea of a local Zanzibar-ian nationalism, encompassing both Africans and Arabs, and the broader issue of African racial solidarity. John Okello after all, was not a Zanzibari at all, but was an imported revolutionary from Uganda. An Africa which strongly objects to white mercenaries in the civil wars in other countries applauded the intervention of a foreign soldier of fortune from Uganda into the history of Zanzibar.

In Mutesa's book, however, what is captured is the equally recurrent theme in Africa of where tribalism ends and nationalism begins. Were the Baganda a nationality? Were the Ibos a nationality? Should the Kingdom of Buganda have enjoyed autonomy in spite of confrontations with the Central Government? There are some background themes which underlie the polemical and defensive book, *The Desecration of My Kingdom* by Sir Edward Mutesa, the former Kabaka of Buganda.

To conclude this section then, it ought to be noted that African biographies in East Africa, perhaps by their very nature as autobiographies, provide an intermediate position between literature and political testament. And there are times when the imagination is as effectively at play in an autobiographical portrayal as it might be in complete fiction.

THE SONG OF SELFHOOD

We indicated earlier Lionel Trilling's conviction of the centrality of selfhood in literature and its relationship to the ideas of Freud and Psychoanalysis. We have also indicated the place of biography in the literary productivity of East Africa, and pointed out the conspicuous fact that much of it is connected with some aspect of Kenya's nationalism and with the Mau Mau Insurrection at large.

As it happens, the same observation is true about the works of East Africa's most prominent novelist, James Ngugi. The theme of Kikuyu self-consciousness and the quest of this people for either collective fulfilment or collective reconciliation are recurrent in Ngugi's fictional works. Ngugi's *The River Between* and *A Grain of Wheat* are, in a sense, within a tradition which includes Kenyatta's work in the 1930s, *Facing Mount Kenya*. The same factors which exposed a theme of negritude in some of the postulates of Kenyatta's analysis of the Kikuyu's tribal life also expose themes of cultural nationalism and its clash with modernizing buoyancy within Ngugi's works of fiction. The simple faith in education – very often Western education as an instrument both for progress and self-preservation is sometimes overpowering. As for female circumcision, it assumes in *The River Between* some of the social significance it commanded at a formative period of nationalism in Kenya. The battle between tradition and modernity, custom and Christianity, find a battleground on the issue of female circumcision. And members of the tribe who want to combine the new with the old sometimes find it psychologically feasible to regard the new as only tenable in terms of the old.

Muthoni said she had seen Jesus. She had done so by going back to the tribe, by marrying the rituals of the tribe with Christ. And she had seen Him through suffering. She had been circumcised and said she had become a woman. Nyambura too wanted to become a woman but she could only be so if Waiyaki talked to her, if he stood near her. Then she would see Christ.[11]

Even Waiyaki later attempts a real reconciliation. At least he is converted to the notion of transition of moving from the old to the new not by an abrupt change, but by the slow curative process of education.

Yes, in the quietness of the hill, Waiyaki had realized many things. Circumcision of women was not important as a physical operation. It is what it did inside a person. It could not be stopped overnight. Patience, and above all, education, was needed.[12]

Muthoni's case illustrates not only the agonies of reconciliation but also the burden of martyrdom in the very attempt to do so. Biblical imagery recurs periodically in Kikuyu nationalism at large. Sometimes it concerns the challenge of forgiveness – the struggle to forgive those fellow Kikuyu who hounded and opposed the Mau Mau. There is an echo of Jesus on the Cross in Josiah Kariuki's attitude towards the former Home Guards when he discusses them in his book '*Mau Mau*' *Detainee*. 'Othaya was not a good camp,' Kariuki tells us. 'If any one was found with snuff he was beaten mercilessly. The wardens there were largely recruited from former Home Guards and, although they hit us so badly, we did not quarrel with them when we were released. We decided that they must be forgiven, for they did not know what they were doing.'[13]

In Ngugi's *A Grain of Wheat* there is a more explicit discussion of the meaning of crucifixion. Is a sacrifice even on the Cross ever worthwhile if it does not encompass in its benefits one's own nation? On the basis of this critical question Kihika, a character in Ngugi's novel, arrives at the conclusion that Christ's sacrifice on the Cross was a failure. It might have saved a lot of people, but it did not save the Jews. It did not serve Jesus' own nation.

Yes – I said he had failed because his death did not change anything, it did not make his people find a centre in the cross. All oppressed people have a cross to bear. . . . Had Christ's death a meaning for the children of Israel? In Kenya we want a death which will change things, that is to say, we want a true sacrifice. But first we have to be ready to carry the

[11] *The River Between* (London, Heinemann, 1965) pp. 117–18.
[12] *The River Between*, p. 163.
[13] '*Mau Mau*' *Detainee*, p. 137.

cross. I die for you, you die for me, we become a sacrifice for one another.
So I can say that you, Karanja, are Christ. I am Christ. Everybody who
takes the Oath of Unity to change things in Kenya is a Christ.[14]

There are occasions of course when it is not the bearer of a new religion
who is crucified but the defender of an old one. Indeed, the martyrs can
sometimes be simply those who are left behind in a wave of conversion to
modernity. The sense of inadequacy felt by the illiterate child in the company of young enthusiastic bookworms, or of the village girl in the company
of urbanized female sophisticates – this sense of inadequacy can itself be a
Cross that bewildered tradition bears in the face of an overpowering
innovation. Okot p'Bitek captures both the bitterness and the bewilder-
ment of this form of martyrdom in his long poem, *Song of Lawino*. A
simple woman married from the village finds herself increasingly inadequate for a husband who was becoming a fanatic to the cult of modernity.
She is losing her hold over him, he has drifted into the arms of a powdered
and lipsticked piece of female modernity. p'Bitek grossly exaggerates the
arrogance of Ocol, the husband who is supposed to heap insults on his
wife and on the tribal roots from which he sprang. Even if you allow for the
fact that Lawino in her anguish sees too much contempt in the acts of her
husband, the feeling nevertheless persists that the poet himself has erred
on the side of excess in his portrayal of Ocol. Ocol's wife laments:

> Ocol tells me
> That I like dirt.
> He says
> *Shea* butter causes
> Skin diseases.
> He says, Acoli adornments
> Are old fashioned and unhealthy.
> He says I soil his white shirt
> If I touch him,
> My husband treats me
> As if I am suffering from
> The 'Don't touch me' disease!
>
> He says that I make his bed-sheets dirty
> And his bed smelly.
> Ocols says
> I look extremely ugly
> When I am fully adorned
> For the dance![15]

[14] *A Grain of Wheat* (London, Heinemann, 1967) p. 110.
[15] *Song of Lawino* (Nairobi: East African Publishing House), p. 58.

If Lawino's account of her husband is correct, Okot has merely succeeded in creating a caricature that could in no way be regarded as representative of the type of person he wants to typify. Ocol by this account is a hyperbolic deserter from his own culture. The person lacks full credibility. On the other hand, if the exaggeration is supposed to be a method of characterizing Lawino's mind rather than of giving us the real picture of her husband, again p'Bitek only succeeds in making Lawino a little too simple. A mind that exaggerates so much and in such an obvious way is a mind which is not simply *culturally* distinct from the modernity which enchants Ocol; it is also a mind too naïve to stand a chance of saving Ocol from that enchantment. The traditional ways of the Acoli deserve a better defender than Lawino in this instance.

But even after making allowances for the exaggerations and superficialities of *Song of Lawino*, it does rank as a major pioneering achievement in East Africa. It is a passionate soliloquy, an utterance of cultural nationalism.

Uganda, in fact, seems to be taking the leadership in this medium of long versified discourse on important themes. Close behind Okot p'Bitek's *Song of Lawino* has emerged also from Uganda Okello Oculi's *Orphan*. Although crude and rough in many parts, there are passages in *Orphan* which are strikingly more profound than anything in *Song of Lawino*. And even commonplace ideas like the cruelty of nature are given renewed evocative power by Oculi.

> The courting grasshopper chirps in a sun bath
> Oblivious to the pangs in the body
> Of a vagabond dog dragging along
> Against the weight of creeping rot in a limb.
> Trapped within the walls of a localized awareness,
> Nature's imposition to justify her . . .
> Indifference to individual pains . . .
> The message in the yell of the goat
> Frightened of the vision behind the slaughter,
> The glassy light in its eyes – unfinished
> Beams left bouncing off the rude opacity
> Of the sudden wall of void eternity;
>
> The melancholy chat of flesh in the cooking pot:
> Only arouse all appetites for heed.
> The disposed-of bones in the homestead,
> Scattered in a jumble, questioned the fate of
> The flesh that once walled their unity
> And sing the credo of the final isolation . . .[16]

[16] *Orphan* (Nairobi, East African Publishing House, 1968) pp. 28–9.

But *Orphan* is not merely an exercise in cultural nationalism, though there are passages within it which are so preoccupied. It is also in many parts a comprehensive indictment of natural cruelty, social injustice, and of the terror of inevitability. The conscience within the poem sometimes shrinks away in horror from the 'Poverty of the man without cows for a wife.'[17]

LITERATURE AND TRANS-NATIONALISM

But it is not merely with the localized dimension of identity that literature concerns itself. There are also moments when feelings of national assertion become intermingled with feelings of international empathy. This is when nationalism broadens its scope and becomes trans-nationalism. It displays capacity to include within itself a link with the world beyond.

In East African literature trans-nationalism sometimes simply takes the form of sympathizing with others in a similar kind of oppressive predicament. At its more immediate level many aspects of Pan-Africanism are, in fact, cases of trans-nationalism. There have been poems about Angola or Sharpeville or, in a different dimension, about the Nigerian Civil War, which have constituted moments of experience in trans-nationalism empathy. Such experiences have on and off been captured within the pages of East African literary magazines. But sometimes their empathetic identification has traversed continents. The second issue of *Zuka*, for example, has a poem by Jonathan Kariara and another by Charles Owuor, both bearing the same title. The title is *'Vietnam'*. Lines from the two poems can be interspersed without disturbing too much the mood of a deep shared depression:

> Women sat reclining
> Monuments of peace
> Sculptured by death.
> The river heaved, eased
> Flowed on . . .
> quiet
> depressing quiet
> sombre quiet of a cathedral
> as mutilated human bodies
> sleep the sleep of ages . . .
> In the field the dead women
> Sighed

[17] *Ibid*, p. 31.

> Remembering the dull thud
> Of the metal fist
> Of the interrogator . . .
> No more, no more
> Betrayal
> The useless pain of snatching
> Life from the fertile flood.[18]

But trans-nationalism does not consist only in identification with other peoples abroad; it also consists in identification with other literatures elsewhere.

Obiajunwa Wali started a controversy in *Transition* sometime ago on whether literature written in the English language was part of English literature or can ever justify a claim to being African literature. Wali himself was convinced no literature written in a European language could claim to be African any more than literature written in, say, Spanish, could claim to be Italian literature. But there were strong voices raised against him, and the discussion continues to be a recurrent theme in literary polemics in Eastern Africa.[19]

Then within the pages of *Zuka* there has been discussion on whether 'abstract verse', encompassing a degree of obscurity which can never claim to have any one meaning, is or is not part of African literary traditions. Christopher Okigbo's poetry especially was cited as being so abstract as to constitute 'a departure from traditional poetry'.

> The dilemma facing African poetry in English is whether or not it should bother to establish a connection with forms of poetic expression in Africa antedating the coming of the English language. . . . Great abstract verse demands a gifted command of words, though not necessarily a command of language. Where meaning is to be conveyed, the intellect needs to be employed. But where beautiful pictures are to be transmitted, the instrument is at best the imagination. Great poetry in African languages is a fusion of the intellect and the imagination. Abstract exercises with verbal pictures is a profound departure from this tradition.[20]

Finally there is the place of translation in this whole phenomenon of the

[18] *Zuka*, No. 2, May 1968, pp. 11, and 14–15.
[19] Wali, 'The dead end of African literature?', *Transition*, Vol. 4, No. 10, September 1963.
[20] See Mazrui, 'Abstract Verse and African Tradition', *Zuka*, No. 1, September 1967; Michael Etherton, 'Christopher Okigbo, A Reply', *Zuka*, No. 2, May 1968; Ian J. Inglis under 'Kazi Moto', *Sunday Nation* (Nairobi) November 26, 1967; and Mazrui, 'Meaning versus Imagery in African Poetry', *Présence Africaine*, Spring 1968.

relationship between African literature and the literary heritage of the outside world. And in this respect it is not simply Jomo Kenyatta who establishes some kind of contact with the stream of negritude; it is also in some other ways Julius Nyerere, the President of Tanzania. Julius Nyerere gains this place not by writing an autobiography, or a political pamphlet, but by translating Shakespeare's *Julius Caesar* into Swahili. And here we find an interesting point of contrast between Nyerere and Senghor. Senghor has said,

> It is a fact that French has made it possible for us to communicate . . . to the world the unheard of message which only we could write. It has allowed us to bring to *universal civilization* a contribution without which the civilization of the twentieth century could not have been universal.[21]

By translating Shakespeare into Swahili Nyerere took what was already a piece of universal civilization – and made it still more universal in an African idiom. For Senghor negritude was served when African literature was effectively expressed in a foreign language like French. For Nyerere, one might say, negritude was equally served when a piece of foreign literature was effectively re-expressed in an African language like Swahili. The latter achievement was, at the minimum, a vindication of an African language as a literary medium.[22]

An undertaking of similar significance has been the Swahili translation of Machiavelli's *The Prince* by Fred Kamoga and Ralph Tanner, published by the East African Publishing House in 1968. *Zuka*, although publishing literary material mainly in English, also tries to include in its pages some work in indigenous African languages. Of particular interest has been the translation in Swahili of a medieval English play *Johan Johan*, originally written by John Heywood, and rendered into the African language by E. A. Ibrek.

As I have argued elsewhere, the tendency to regard translation as something distinct from creativity rests on a forced dichotomy. The task of translating world masterpieces into African languages is bound to enrich the creative versatility of the African languages themselves. Nyerere's translation of *Julius Caesar* has contributed more to the potential of Swahili as a *dramatic* medium than almost any original work in Swahili which has so far emerged.

The enrichment of African languages through their extensive use in both translation and original works must therefore itself be regarded as a nationalistic aspiration of wide influence.

---

[21] 'Negritude and the concept of Universal Civilisation', *Présence Africaine*, Vol. 18, No. 46, Second Quarter, 1963, p. 310.
[22] See the Chapter 'Symbolism of Julius Caesar' in Mazrui, *The Anglo-African Commonwealth* (Oxford, Pergamon Press, 1967).

CONCLUSION

We have tried to demonstrate here that the relationship between national-ism and literature in Africa, with special reference to East Africa, has three intellectual strata. There is first the very act of putting pen to paper in an imaginative way. The newness of literary culture among some African societies has helped to give creative writing as an activity a nationalistic prestige of its own.

The second level of relationship between nationalism and literature in this region concerns the themes which are treated in African works. The portrayal of heroic moments in East African history, either through bio-graphy or fiction, is often an attempt to define clouds of glory behind the trail of African nationalism. The defence of tradition against modernity, of the indigenous against the foreign, is a song of self-identity which has echoed down the centuries and traversed different cultures. It has its place in the biography, fiction and poetry of East Africa.

Finally, we discussed the dimension of relationship between a national literature and the global literary heritage of the world. This is the moment of transition from nationalism to trans-nationalism. The political themes which are treated in this kind of literature are sometimes passionate exercises of empathetic identification with others abroad. The agony of Angola or Vietnam stings onlookers half-a-culture or seven cultures away.

But what of the literature which deals with corruption among African politicians after independence? What of the fiction of military coups? What of Achebe's *Man of the People* and Rubadiri's *No Bride Price*? Is this a post-nationalistic literature? Indeed, is this the moment of disenchant-ment with nationalism?

It is more a moment of disenchantment with *the first fruit* of nationalism – an entirely different form of reaction. To be disappointed with the first harvest of one's little plot of land is not necessarily the end of one's love for the land, or of one's faith in its future. An indictment of political corrup-tion in post-independence Africa can itself be a form of nationalism. Wole Soyinka regards a social conscience as an integral part of African art in its primordial form. In his own words:

> When the writer in his own society can no longer function as a conscience he must recognize that his choice lies between denying himself totally or withdrawing to the position of chronicler and post-mortem surgeon. . . . The artist has always functioned in African society as the record of mores and experience of his society *and* as the voice of vision in his own time. It is time for him to respond to this essence of himself.

In East Africa the disillusion with the first fruit of independence is not as yet acute. The region has not (as yet?) experienced the political, moral and military excesses which have agonized parts of West Africa already since independence. But the literature of social conscience is beginning to emerge in East Africa as well. And through it a new meeting point between nationalism and literature would find its way into East African experience too. When that happens East African nationalism would not consist simply in tracing the clouds of glory which lie in the trail of the fatherland. It would also consist in raising the alarm against the dark clouds of impending storm on the horizon of nationhood.

There was a time when to criticize Africa had connotations of disloyalty. Perhaps never again would it be quite as easy to distinguish between a song of African patriotism and the anguished choke of African self-indictment.

S. Okechukwu Mezu

▼▼▼▼▼▼▼▼▼▼▼▼▼▼▼▼▼▼▼▼▼▼▼▼▼▼▼▼▼

Poetry and Revolution in Modern Africa
[1970]

IN the words of the late Dame Edith Sitwell, 'poetry is the light of the Great Morning wherein the beings whom we see passing in the street are transformed for us into the epitome of all beauty, or of all joy, or of all sorrow'. Poetry is therefore a part of human life and does not have to be written and in fact for a long time, African poetry was mainly oral and unwritten. In the African village, travelling bards sang songs and recited poetry to the accompaniment of musical instruments. These bards told stories and anecdotes. Some of these recitals were serious and historical bringing into light the events of war and peace with occasional commentary on the reigns of various chiefs and strong men of the village. Others were lyrical while a few were coarse and bawdy. But most of them were roundelays and quite often people joined in the narration.

Among the Igbos, for instance, on occasions like the *Yam Festival*, the village bard leads the dancing group with incantations. His songs are poetic in composition and are filled with refrains. The tonal nature of some of these languages in Africa adds more rhythm and pulse to the recitations while the drum in the background provides the necessary mood and atmosphere. In the morning and at dusk, the libation of the Igbo elder to his gods is an interesting mixture of prayer and poetry. The prayer is natural, the poetry spontaneous and he creates both as he gives his humble offerings to the gods as is seen in this prayer:

Ala	— Earth
Nụrụ mmee	— Receive (my) libation
Ọfọ na Ogu	— Curses and Justice
Nụrụ mmee	— Receive (my) libation
Ala ukwu Emeke	— Great Earth of Emeke
Nụrụ mmee	— Receive (my) libation
Ọfọ egbu ji	— Curses do not destroy yams
Ọfọ egbu ede	— Curses do not destroy coco-yams
Emere nini ji egbu ọfọ	— Clear conscience disarms curses

The Igbo elder addresses his god in this poetic form and in moments of intense joy, sorrow, satisfaction or even frustration, he tries to capture his rapture or despair with some form of poetic expression. Meeting you on the road, the Igbo villager, on his way to the farm early in the morning greets the passer-by and quite often the following dialogue ensues:

Ị bọ-ọla chi?	— Are you awake?
Eh, ngi kwanu?	— Yes and you?
Anyi abo-ola, Ndi uyo gi kwanu?	— We are awake and your house?
Ha abọ-ọla, ndi, nke gi kwanu?	— They are awake and yours?
Ha afutala.	— They have come out
Ụmụaka kwanu?	— And the children?
Ha nu, ma ndi nke gi?	— They exist and yours?
Ha nuisiri ike	— They are strong and there

Before the villager arrives at his farm, the chances are that he would go through this ritual several times. This repetition, with nuances, with little variations, in greetings is found not only in life itself but in African music, dance and poetry, all of which are interrelated. A similar greeting among the Sereres of Senegal runs like a litany, as this passage translated into French by Léopold Senghor illustrates:

As-tu la paix?	— Do you have peace?
La paix seulement	— Peace only
Ton pere a-t-il la paix?	— Your father does he have peace?
La paix seulement	— Peace only
Ta mere a-t-elle la paix?	— Your mother does she have peace?
La paix seulement	— Peace only
Les gens de ta maison ont-ils la paix?	— The people of your household do they also have peace?
La paix seulement	— Peace only

According to Leopold Senghor the villager continues to ask about the parents, the relations, the friends, the farms, the cattle of his interlocutor. They talk about past experiences, about friends they have in common as joy or sorrow hangs over their faces. They embrace one another and shake hands for a long time. Suddenly, the salutations begin again. 'Cette fois, sur un rythme aux aretes plus nettes, sur le rythme meme du poeme qui tend la poitrine, serre la gorge, exprime l'emotion. C'est alors que l'on eclate en sanglots, que coulent de grosses larmes'.[1]

In the villages of Africa, dances are held periodically and most of the tunes are made up of poetic verses. In the evenings, when children

[1] Léopold Sédar Senghor, 'Elements constitutifs d'une civilisation d'inspiration negro-africaine', *Liberté I : Negritude et Humanisme*, Paris, Seuil, 1964, p. 260.

gather to listen to stories, yarns and fairy-tales from their grandparents, they listen to pieces interspersed with rhymes, lyrics and choruses. Everyone takes part in the recitation. Those who do not know the words, hum the tune and as people clap there is a happy union of music, harmony and poetry. Songs, music and poems are also used effectively to create the desired atmosphere and evoke the appropriate emotion on other solemn, happy or sorrowful occasions. The emphasis is on the participation of everyone. There is generally a communal approach to poetry. During ceremonies commemorating the birth of a child, lyrics are sung all night by women. On the eve of her wedding, the young bride is accompanied to her fiancé's home by members of her sex and age. Poetry and music formed part of the ceremony. On the death of a renowned villager, the local cantor leads the group of mourners with his chants. During the elegy, the cantor invokes the glorious dead, laments the departed citizen and sings his praises pointing out some of his achievements in life. While the body of the deceased still lies in state, young men and women stay up all night, wake and sing songs. Often these are composed extemporaneously, stanza by stanza. Everyone participates. When an individual feels that he has created a verse, a stanza or even a line that fits into the dirge, he simply takes to the floor and sings his new verse. The new stanza if good is adopted and becomes part of the repertoire. *Generally in African society, poetry was not the monopoly of a few professional scribblers, but a common heritage shared by all and handed over from generation to generation.*

Poetry was an integral part of the life of the people. Hence some of the poems dealt with local scandals. The African village traditionally was a small unit where every inhabitant knew about, and was interested in, the affairs of his neighbour. If there were any case of petty larceny or even pregnancy, a lyric was immediately composed to focus attention on the incident. The little poem very often composed by a mischievous urchin, grows longer and more sarcastic as it rolls from one village to another. Such was the nature and form of African poetry in its oral stage and like the poetry of other peoples, it was recited and sung long before people thought of putting it down in black and white.

One of the most interesting aspects of traditional African civilization is the unity of the art forms. It seems that there is fully realized the great *correspondance* dream of Charles Baudelaire – the unity and association of music, poetry, dance and painting in the process of which the sounds of music, the rhythms, phrases and syllables, the allegories and analogies of poetry, the steps, movements, jumps and signals of dance and finally the colours of painting are unified in a symbolic world where religion provides a solid and firm structure. Side by side with this unity of the art forms is the element of repetition which incidentally is found also in black American music especially in jazz and blues, where slight and endlessly variable permutations and combinations lend novelty and continuity to the trumpets of a Louis Armstrong or where the languorous, melancholic and ever fading voice of a Ray Charles holds the listener spell-bound as he follows the unfolding rhythm of blues. The same repetition is also found in cha-cha, the samba, the pachanga, rhumba, maringa and the popular West African high-life. This repetitive approach to most African art forms, a litany that says the same thing in various ways, describing the attributes of the object of praise in an unfathomable way is akin to the European surrealist conception of poetry and art. In fact, André Breton and his group instinctively looked up to those societies not yet atomized and objectivized by modern techniques and technology for individual and collective salvation. They were in search of the unity of African art form. They searched for societies not yet infected by the speed and materialism of modern life, lands where dream and life, the world beyond the plain realities of life below have not yet been divorced or set in opposition, one against the other.

In traditional African society, the arts, poetry, music, dance are not usually carried out for their own sake. The Parnassian concept of art in the manner of Leconte de Lisle, that is to say, art for art's own sake, is not a valid thesis in the African system. Neither can one rightly posit a purely religious interpretation of African arts. Stendhal, for instance, wrote his novels for the 'happy few'. Such literature is out of place in traditional African culture. So too would the elegant hermetism of Mallarmé or the poetry of Ezra Pound. African poetry traditionally was not meant for a few bards. The *griots*, very common in Moslem parts of black Africa, must of necessity be excluded. These are courtesans paid to chant the glories of a chief or king, to praise him in front of an assembly, to flatter him because the griot's employer wants to beg a favour of the king. This appears to be a degradation of the village bard, whose profession, if it can be called such, was a serious and an honourable one – that of leading his people in a collective expression of joy or sorrow. Sycophancy and court poetry as practised more recently in history by the griots of Senegal for instance appears to be far removed from the traditional tenor of African music and poetry. Poetry was conceived as a collective work wherein participate various peoples. Hermetism is out of the question. If there are complex symbols, these are usually within the reach of the age-group, the initiated group, the tribe or the community. If the symbols are not easily accessible to the lay man it is because a cabalistic group or the initiated members of a fraternity want to guard some of their secrets or cults. Otherwise the poetry featuring during ceremonies dealing with birth, initiation, marriage, wedding, death and burial was within the reach of the group concerned.

Traditionally very little distinction is made between songs and poetry.

Even stories and tales are poetic in form and nature. Most pieces of music are lyrical or poetic and music itself, like poetry, is finalistic. Music for mere relaxation or enjoyment is foreign to the African village just as parnassian poetry is not traditional to his nature. When there is music, it usually is meant for a dance, and quite often when there is poetry it usually is meant to be sung. The traditional African would have a hard time appreciating a performance of works of Beethoven, Wagner or Bach whether in a chamber music set up or in a full dress orchestral performance where the audience listens in mournful silence, quite often half asleep, only to clap at the end aroused by the general burst of applause. But the African villager might probably appreciate an opera by Wagner or Verdi, but most certainly if he can from the auditorium, from the floor, physically take part in it, adding a few lines to the poetry and a few movements to the dance. In London or Washington, the Cinema theatre is a dead place interspersed with the crack of popcorn and the methodical slaughter of spearmint gum. In Lagos or Accra, in the theatre, in the cinema house, each movement in the film is spontaneously and instantly appraised by the crowd – as in Shakespearian theatres, as in the Romanistic theatre of nineteenth-century France. The audience in the African tradition takes part, a full and lively part in the performance. An Indian prince kissing the cheeks of a dreaming princess in a romantic garden of roses might be greeted with a spontaneous and hilarious shout by the audience of 'Ehh....' coupled with a swinging motion of the body. An American cowboy film, featuring a mock boxing scene might be greeted with short stabbing shouts of 'Eh! ... Eh!! ... Eh! ...' and a long one 'Kpoo ... ooooo....' as the hero floors his opponent. Traditionally, the African spectator of a music performance, a dance exhibit or poetry reading has to feel and participate at least emotionally in the situation for it to have a real significance for him.

African traditional poetry can therefore be described as a collective experience initiated by an individual in a group and shared by the rest. It is a conscious and finalistic attempt to verbalize, vocalize or orchestrate notions, themes and/or events for enjoyment, parody, or veneration with a view to artistic creation, group catharsis or supernatural contemplation. Thus modern African poetry written in English, French, Spanish or Portuguese, is a marked departure from the poetic tradition of African literature. Yet the new poetry has something in common with the old.

Modern African poetry has become personal. It is no longer a collective experience, a collective exploration. Because the modern poet has had to write in English, French, Spanish or Portuguese, the language problem has greatly modified his ability to speak to his people, to share his experiences with them. *From a group catharsis, modern African poetry became an experiment in self-exorcism. Because he can no longer speak to his people, the*

*modern African poet unconsciously has chosen to speak for them, to represent
them as it were on the contemporary scene.* Because traditionally, poetry was a
part of the life of the people, the modern poet has chosen to deal with those
preoccupations of his people at this juncture in history. The modern
African poet has chosen to sing, chant, shout, be angry, rave, curse,
condemn and praise when occasion demands it in the interests of his
people. Because his people's preoccupations are of a revolutionary nature,
African poetry recently, contrary to traditional poetry, has by and large
been revolutionary. Because modern black Africa has been faced with the
problem of decolonization, the African poet has come out in full force to
defend the oppressed and to condemn the oppressor. Because modern
Africa has been faced with the problem of racism and racial apartheid, the
poet has come out with vehemence to defend his people and to condemn
the racists. Because Africa is concerned with the bastardization of the black
continent, some African poets have raised up their voices to defend the
traditional culture and condemn the Westernization of their homeland.
Because black Africa is concerned with the situation of the black people in
the United States, poets in Africa have raised their voices to sing the black
man's right to be free. So if there is one dominant theme in African life
today, it is that of revolt and this revolution appears to have found adequate
expression in African poetry. Revolution is a dynamic process and is ever
evolving. This explains why what was revolutionary poetry thirty years ago
may today be considered by some as a reactionary philosophy.

This particularly is the case with the movement called negritude in
poetry. Thirty years ago, it was revolutionary for the black poet to proclaim
from roof-top the beauty of the black woman, the black world, as Léopold
Senghor did in his poem 'Femme noire, femme nue'. Before the Second
World War, Africa was still considered a *terra incognita*. Thus the black poet,
of African descent, the West Indian Aimé Cesaire, in his *Cahier d'un
retour au pays natal,* had to defend these black peoples that the white world
accused of having discovered nothing, invented nothing, created nothing:

> Those who invented neither powder nor compass
> those who never tamed steam or electricity
> those who did not explore sea or sky
>   but they know in their innermost depths the
> country of suffering
> those who knew of voyages only when uprooted
> those who are made supple by kneelings
> those domesticated and Christianized
> those inoculated with degeneracy
> tom-toms of empty hands

> tom-toms of sounding wounds
> burlesque tom-toms of treason.

Leon Damas, also a West Indian black, felt compelled in his *Pigments*, a volume of poetry to defend the black continent. His poems were so powerful and the message so direct that his book was banned because at his instigation, the people of Ivory Coast refused to be mobilized by the French in 1939, mobilized to fight to liberate France that was keeping them under subjugation in their own homeland. The Senegalese David Diop spoke out in his *Coups de pilon* against the new Africa that was being created by white colonialists, financiers and industrialists. In his poem, 'Afrique', he contrasts the present with the old Africa of proud warriors in the ancestral savannah as chanted by his mother. He never knew that Africa. Before him he sees Africa of the slave trade, of forced labour and wasted pains, Africa humble and humiliated.

We basically hear the same accents in the poem of Paul Niger, 'Je n'aime pas l'Afrique', again the Africa that is exploited:

> Africa is going to speak
> Because it is her turn now to make her demands:
>   'I wanted a land where men were men
> and not wolves
> and not sheep
> and not serpents
> and not camelions
> I wanted a land where the land was land
> Where harvest was harvest'
> . . . .
> Africa is going to speak
> Africa with a single justice and with a single crime
> Crime against God, the crime against men
> Crime against royal Africa
> Crime against those who own something
> What?
> Rhythm.

Also Bernard Dadié of the Ivory Coast in a very strident voice, after a brief imprisonment for political reasons by the colonial government, adds another dimension to the revolutionary voice of Paul Niger. With the accents of Paul Eluard's well-known poem 'Hymne à la liberté', Bernard Dadié professes his 'Fidelité à l'Afrique':

> From the public square
> From the floor of the Tribunal

On the naked grounds of humid prisons
>Everyone
I will tell them, what they are, these extortioners
And even if in their furor
They cut off my head
>My blood
So that they can read it always
Will write in the heavens
'Fidelity to Africa'.

Bernard Dadié is talking about fidelity to Africa of the tam-tam, Africa of joyful young girls, happy peasants working communally Dadié is talking about Africa of happy nights filled with songs, the land which according to the Ivoirian poet has now been taken over by the kings of petrol and iron, the princes of diamond and gold, the barons of wood and rubber. He is speaking of the Africa that is gradually losing its peasants who are being replaced by famished factory workers, exhausted plantation workers, buried, when they die, in common graves.

Léopold Senghor in his poem, a dramatic poem, 'Chaka' is even more specific in his condemnation of this process of exploitation. The voice is that of Chaka betrayed by his people and on the point of death. In a vision he sees beyond his reign and after his death, all the countries bounded by the four cardinal points, in Africa that is, subjected to the rule and compass of the white man. The woods will be deforested and hills levelled, rivers and valleys will be subjected to destructive exploration. The railroad will draw double lines across the continent and the people of the South, the former Zulu kingdom, will work like ants silent and exploited. There was a time when work was considered sacred and holy and noble, but, the voice of Chaka continues, labour in the future will never be the same. The element of volition will have gone, the voice of the tam-tam will be silent. The people of South Africa will work no longer for themselves, but in the factories, in the ports, docks, mines and industries for other people. At night, they will go back to their segregated kraals of misery. During the day, black people, the voice of Chaka continues, will amass for other people mountains of black gold, red gold (signifying the blood of black people) for other people, while they themselves die of hunger at dusk. Finally Chaka speaks of this vision of his people humiliated, famished, with withered arms, stomach caved in, bulging eyes and lips calling upon an impossible god. And in a rhetorical question, Chaka, whom Senghor himself presented as a poet and politician, asked: 'Can I remain silent in the face of such unredeemed suffering?' Basically it is the same question each African poet asks himself. It is what leads the African poet also to take up his people's cry of revolt,

revolt against injustice, revolt against exploitation. The sorrow is evident in these words of Chaka: 'They wanted merchandise, we gave them everything: ivory, honey, rainbow coloured skin; spices, gold, precious stones, parrots and monkeys, just name it!' Naturally they were not satisfied. And the voice of revolution continued, proclaiming in the process the preoccupations of the people.

Still recently from South Africa comes the voice of Dennis Brutus who was largely responsible for South Africa's exclusion from the Olympic Games. Arrested in 1963, he tried to escape twice but was recaptured and sentenced to eighteen months of imprisonment with hard labour where he was not allowed to write poetry for publication. But he succeeded in writing his 'Letters to Martha', narrating his experiences: 'In prison the clouds assume importance and the birds with a small space of sky cut off by the walls of black hostility and pressed upon by hostile authority the mind turns upwards when it can.' The reader hears the thudding boots of the guard leaving his machine-gun post to find out what is amiss in the prison cell. In another poem by Dennis Brutus entitled 'The Mob' referring to the white crowd who attacked those protesting on the steps of the Johannesburg City Hall against the Sabotage Bill in May 1962, the same story is told:

> These are the faceless horrors
> that people my nightmares
> from whom I turn to wakefulness
> for comforting
> . . . .
> O my people
> O my people
> what have you done
> and where shall I find comforting
> to smooth awake your mask of fear
> restore your face, your faith, feeling tears.

The cry sounds very much like that in the Old Testament where the prophet cried: 'Popule meus! Popule meus! Quid feci tibi? Responde mihi,' a passage usually sung during ceremonies commemorating the passion of Christ on Good Friday. But for the black world it appears to be a perennial, a perpetual passion. And the voices of protest continue: – O my people, O my people! What have I done to you? Please answer me. The people in question is humanity at large but more specifically the white world.

Also with the advent of literacy in Africa, the traditional lyrics and poems were not only transcribed but a few were translated into English or

French. For instance, Adeboye Babalola has translated the poems of Yoruba hunters (Ijala) into English blank verse. Rems Nna Umeasiegbu, in his work, *The Way We Lived*, has also translated a significant number of Igbo customs and stories. Léopold Senghor, Birago Diop, Bernard Dadié have done similar things in the francophone world.

Basically, poetry expressed the needs and feelings of the people and as these needs and feelings changed, shifted and expanded, the theme of African poetry also grew. Naturally the agitation for Independence in the political field gave rise to nationalist poetry, poems that invoked the inviolability of the African continent, its territorial integrity. At some time or other in their life, either in schools in foreign countries or in prison in their home countries, African leaders of the independence era have written poems to epitomize their struggle for political and cultural liberation. Dennis Osadebay of Nigeria, one of the first in that country to publish a volume of poetry has this to write in 'Who Buys My Thoughts':

>Who buys my thoughts
>Buys not a cup of honey
>That sweetens every taste;
>He buys the throb,
>Of Young Africa's soul,
>The soul of teeming millions,
>Hungry, naked, sick,
>Yearning, pleading, waiting.

Also David Rubadiri, a Malawi educator, poet and once his country's Ambassador to Washington, D.C. writes in the same vein in one of his college poems entitled 'The Tide That From the West Washes Africa to the Bones'. It is an angry voice of protest, of revolution such that one hears the tides of Western culture and domination buffeting the skeletal form of Africa:

>The tide that from the West
>Washes Africa to the bones
>Gargles through my ribs
>Gathers the bones clustering
>Rough and polished
>To fling them back destitute
>To the river bank
>The tide that from the West
>Washes the soul of Africa,
>Washes the buoys of its spirits
>Tears the mooring apart
>Till blood red the tide becomes

And heartsick the wounds.
The tide that from the West
Washes Africa
Once, washed a wooden cross.

In the face of continued colonialism in places like Angola, Mozambique
and Spanish Guinea and in other areas dominated by a white minority
government as in Rhodesia and South Africa, voices are still heard singing
of human dignity and the rights of man to determine his destiny. Even in
areas where independence had been achieved, there was also a slight shift
of emphasis in its poetry. Instead of decrying colonialism, African poets
tried to sing the glory of the past. Africa in search of an identity, a personality, tried to illustrate that Africa has a culture rich and vital and glorious
enough to match if not supersede the cultures of the nations that have
colonized them. Symbolic at least of this kind of feeling is the volume of
poetry, *Songs of Africa*, published in 1961 by M. O. Okogie, of Nigeria.
In his introduction, he says: 'I observe that European poets set into poetry
ideas of their native customs and culture. This delights me. I love Milton's
Lycidas; Wadsworth's *Yarrow Unvisited and Yarrow Visited*; and Scott's
The Lady of the Lake. They are a source of inspiration to me. Africa, too,
has much native custom and culture which lends itself to imaginative
poetry.' Okogie goes on to say that '*Songs of Africa* is a volume of poetry
with a purely African background. It is no imitation; it contains no
political eulogy; it is by itself and it is second to none.' Okogie seems to
suggest that the time for political eulogies and deprecations was coming to
an end. The aim he set for himself was the illustration of the great wealth
of the African culture. He does exactly this in his poem, 'There is Love in
Hair-Plaiting', where he describes the beauty of Nigerian women. These
women are noted particularly for the variety of their hair styles which,
Okogie writes, becomes even more beautiful 'on the head of the girl of
your love'.

But the racial element, another African and black preoccupation continued in Africa's poetry. Already African poets following after the
Americans like Langston Hughes and Jean Toomer and Countee Cullen
tried also to show that there was beauty and pride in blackness, in being
black and having Africans as one's ancestors. African poets sang and
praised the black woman, her ebony skin. They also glorified the mascu-
linity of the black man. Negritude which Jean-Paul Sartre described as an
anti-racist racism by far dominated African poetry, at least certain sections
of it, and the cult of beauty black and African caught the admiration of the
world. This sentiment was already exemplified in Leopold Senghor's
classic poem, 'Femme noire', where he addresses African womanhood:

naked woman, dark woman, symbol of life and maturity, whose colour symbolizes life itself, and whose form is nothing but beauty as jewels sparkle like stars on the darkness of her skin. For a long time afterwards this image of the black woman became a new idol worthy of veneration by the African poet.

Langston Hughes in his book *An African Treasury* has compared this accent on blackness to the racial consciousness found in the work of American Negro writers not too long ago. 'The Harlem writers of that period,' writes Hughes, 'had to search for their folk roots. The African writer has these roots at hand.' This sentiment which in people like Senghor is lyrical and a cult of beauty, black and African, takes more poignant dimensions in the works of poets like Francis Kobina Parkes of Ghana. In his poem, 'Apocalypse' he writes:

> In the last days
> Strange sights shall visit the earth.
> Sights that may turn to blood the moon,
> This sun to midnight – in the last days.

In another poem, 'African Heaven', Francis Kobina Parkes makes clear his intention:

> Give me black souls
> Let them be black
> Or chocolate brown
> Or make them the
> Colour of dust –
> Dustlike,
> Browner than sand.
> But if you can
> Please keep them black,
> Black.

Elsewhere there are words of hope and inspiration to the peoples of Africa and of African descent in the words of the Ghanaian Michael Dei-Anang:

> Dark Africa
> My dawn is here
> Behold, I see
> A rich-warm glow in the East
> And my day will soon be here.

But in spite of this prophecy of the rising sun in Africa, a sort of *tropical dawn,* perhaps an African version of the *Celtic Twilight* that saw the ascendancy of William Butler Yeats, there are other poets lamenting at about the same time, in a revolutionary sort of way the passing of the old and the traditional. Abioseh Nicol's poetry falls in this category of the poetry of regret, regret of the past and a criticism of the present, the growing influence of Western culture and the sometimes nefarious impact of the same on Africa. There is the desire of *re-evolution* to the past since villages are being replaced by cities and huts are giving way to sky-scrapers and independent farmers are being turned into famished factory workers. Often, though, this condemnation of the new is not followed by an alternative. Often the bemoaning of the loss of the old is not followed with concrete and positive steps to preserve the disappearing. In his poem 'Up-Country', Abioseh Nicol writes:

> Then I came back
> Sailing down the Guinea Coast,
> Loving the sophistication
> Of your brave new cities:
> Dakar, Accra, Cotonou,
> Lagos, Bathurst, and Bisau,
> Freetown, Libreville
> Freedom is really in the mind.
> Go up-country, they said
> To see the real Africa
> For whomsoever you may be,
> That is where you come from,
> Go for bush – inside the bush
> You will find your hidden heart,
> Your mute ancestral spirit.
> And so I went
> Dancing on my way.

This Orphic vision or descent is common with several African poets. Léopold Senghor's poetry is a perpetual quest for the lost fatherland, a perpetual return to the motherland. Symbolic of this tendency is his work in his poem 'Retour de l'Enfant prodige', the return to Africanity, to Africa, of the prodigal son after ten years of errantry in the schools, libraries, and philosophical world of Europe. Césaire's *Cahier d'un retour au pays natal*, can also be seen as an intellectual return to the past. In the two cases, the two poets, like Abioseh Nicol are going 'up-country', 'a la brousse', to the lands untouched, yet, by European materialism. They are going back in search of the edenic kingdom of the old, in search of personal and collective salvation in a world in which they feel more and more alienated and less and less wanted.

One must recognize also the feeling of oneness that Africans have with American blacks, their common and shared heritage and objectives, their common fight against injustice and for the dignity of the black man. This feeling also permeates some of African poetry. It is also evident in the works of American writers. Apart from the well-known writers like Langston Hughes, Claude McKay, William Du Bois, one reads, for instance in the November–December, 1964, issue of *African Opinion* (New York) a poem entitled 'Before it's too late' by Kattie Cumboo. The poem illustrates the tendency of the African and the black American to view their cultural and political aspirations as one and inseparable:

> AFRICA,
> my heart cries out to thee
> please come
> and rescue me:
> AFRICA,
> I'm drowning in a pool
> of bigotry
> and hate
> please come.
> Africa
> before it's too late.

Twenty years earlier this unity of feeling and interest was underscored in the poem of Léopold Senghor dedicated 'To the American Negro Troops':

> Behold your strong face, I did not recognize you
> Yet I had only to touch the warmth of your
>   dark hand – my name is *Africa*!
> And I discovered lost laughter again,
>   and heard old voices, and the roaring rapids
> of the Congo.

The revolutionary stage of African poetry appears however to be fading at least from the continental point of view. Certainly revolutionary poems will continue to emerge from events like the Biafran War, the Sudanese struggle, and the guerrilla warfare going on in Portuguese controlled areas. However negritude and other currents as practised before independence are already dated. *With the achievement of at least token independence creative writing is gradually shifting from the contemplation, examination and criticism of the O THER, usually the white expatriate, to an analysis, critique and reflection of the SELF,* usually the black leader, writer or politician. Another kind of poetry is being born, less revolutionary, less collective, more personal, introspective and perhaps unfortunately bourgeois. There are those of us who however think that African poetry should not just be a reactionary movement, that African poetry should not be a religious or political or even a philosophical apologetics. There are those of us who maintain that we should adopt a more positive attitude towards African culture. The neo-African poet sees people as living entities and not as helpless toys caught up in a tumultuous cultural swirl. Without lamentation, undue regrets, apologies, the neo-African poet tries to praise, glorify and preserve in his own little and individual way Africa's cultural heritage. It is true that we should write about the sufferings under the colonial government, the humiliation of our brothers in South Africa, and the continuing struggle by black people in America. The African poet may justifiably write about these events he feels and senses but he must do something more. His writing must be something positive, with a positive message and not a cultural apology in the guise of poetry.

This generation whose experiences appear to be radically different from those of their forerunners appears to have arrived. John Pepper Clark can in his 'Agbor Dancer' celebrate the charm and the rhythm of traditional music and dancing without fanfare and apologies. Wole Soyinka in 'The Immigrant, another immigrant' can look at himself with concern and detachment, with love and irony. Elsewhere in the 'Telephone Conversation', Wole Soyinka writes:

> The price seemed reasonable, location
> Indifferent. The landlady swore she lived
> Off premises. Nothing remained
> But self-confession. 'Madam,' I warned,
> 'I hate a wasted journey – I am African.'
> Silence. Silenced transmission of
> Pressurized good-breeding. Voice, when it came,
> Lipstick coated, long gold-rolled
> Cigarette-holder pipped. Caught I was, foully.
> 'HOW DARK?' ... I had not misheard ... 'ARE
>   YOU LIGHT
> OR VERY DARK?' Button B. Button A. Stench
> Of rancid breath of public hide-and-speak.
> Red booth. Red pillar-box. Red double-tiered
> Omnibus squelching tar. It *was* real! Shamed
> By ill-mannered silence, surrender
> Pushed dumbfounded to beg simplification.
> Considerate she was, varying the emphasis –
> 'ARE YOU DARK? OR VERY LIGHT?' Revelation came.
> 'You mean – like plain or milk chocolate?'

From the above poem it becomes evident that a new kind of revolution is taking place in African poetry. Wole Soyinka here is talking about the discrimination in housing that African students suffer in England. There is the local colour of realism, the double-decked buses, the old red telephone booths. But the irony is a quiet one. The poet no longer raves about injustice, about discrimination. The words do not even appear in the poem. It is a far cry from the violent emotions of Bernard Dadié, Léopold Senghor, Aimé Césaire, David Diop and Leon Damas. The approach here is perhaps too sophisticated, too subtle. There is no lamentation of the old. In fact, the poet seems to have accepted the new. There is no feeling of anger, of harshness but rather one of pity for the landlady, in a way, a prisoner of the racist mores of her society. Quiet irony that mocks at the self and the other with equal objectivity. The new African poet by recording faithfully what he sees, by praising the deserving aspects of the traditional culture and pointing out its weak points, will help towards the preservation of Africa's mores and culture, more so perhaps than all the lamentations about negritude and all the tirades against the Westernization of the black continent.

The general tendency seems to be towards a new romanticism in African poetry, a personal kind of concourse with nature. In Okogbule Wonodi's 'Icheke: IV', there are these lines:

> We fell into the river,
> splashing the water
>   on the riverweeds;
> we heard the rushing of water,
> smelt the offshore farmtime ashes
> and heard the offshore farmtime songs.
> We moved with the currents
> showing kola-free teeth . . .

This is true also of the poetry of Michael Echeruo. In 'Lullaby', it is not the African and the West in conflict with one another, but rather nature in harmony with herself. In a way, there is a new discovery of the past and the traditional, but not the idealized past or the romanticized traditional, but simply the charming realities of contemporary life in a traditional African setting. Michael Echeruo writes:

> now the sun goes down
> into the valley
> beyond the palms;
> the broods will be returning.
> soon the last cock will crow,

> the last clay-pot be stowed,
> and the fifth finger licked.
> sheep and dogs and kids
> beside the hearth
> sleep beyond all reproach.

Some people see in this romantic revival, in the modern versification or lack of versification, the influence of contemporary European poets. This is probably true but above all the new tendency should be seen as a radical break with the dominant trend in African poetry. What this poetry has lost in revolutionary fervour it has certainly gained in charming realism. Christopher Okigbo also wrote in this vein in his poem 'Idoto' from *Heavensgate*:

> Before you, mother Idoto,
>   naked I stand,
> before your watery presence,
>   a prodigal,
> leaning on an oilbean;
> lost in your legend . . .
> Under your power wait I on barefoot,
> Watchman for the watchword at
>   HEAVENSGATE;
> out of the depths my cry
> give ear and hearken.

This tendency in African poetry is spreading and Matei Markwei of Ghana seems to be guided by the same influence, a bit difficult to define. In his simple poem, 'Life in our Village', he gives a positive message with universal dimensions. Again there is no effort to romanticize the past or to condemn the present. The dominating theme seems to be a reconciliation with the environment, its beauty and simplicity, its hypocrisy and irony:

> In our little village
> When elders are around
> Boys must not look at girls
> And girls must not look at boys
> Because the elders say
> That is not good.
> Even when night comes
> Boys must play separately
> Girls must play separately
> But humanity is weak
> So boys and girls meet.

The boys play hide and seek
And the girls play hide and seek
The boys know where the girls hide
And the girls know where the boys hide
So in their hide and seek
Boys seek girls
Girls seek boys
And each to each sing
Songs of love.

Three eras are already perceptible in the evolution of African poetry. Firstly the pre-colonial tradition which was collective and which involved the participation of the individual villager in the collective expression of joys, sorrows, anger, hatred, or even pious sentiments. This era was supplanted by the colonial era during which poetry moved away from the community partly because of linguistic difficulties and the new medium of expression, English, French, Spanish or Portuguese. But the divorce was not total because the poet continued to be actively involved – quite often as a leader and reformer – in the affairs of his people and thus expressed their sense of frustration and revolt against oppression in his poetry. However, with the break in this negative bond of union – colonialism giving way to independence – very little appears now to tie the poet to his people. The post-independence poetry thus tends to be personal rather than collective, introspective rather than revolutionary. But even then the divorce from the people is not complete because the poet seems to derive a new source of inspiration from traditional sources and from his people. But he is no longer expressing their collective unconscious as the travelling bard of the pre-colonial times used to and neither is he speaking on their behalf as the revolutionary poet of the colonial times did. He is simply writing as an individual alone in an existential world, expressing ideas that strike a chord once in a while in the hearts of his people.

Lewis Nkosi

▼▼▼▼▼▼▼▼▼▼▼▼▼▼▼▼▼▼▼▼▼▼▼▼▼▼▼▼▼▼

Fiction by Black South Africans

[1966]

WITH the best will in the world it is impossible to detect in the fiction of black South Africans any significant and complex talent which responds with both the vigour of the imagination and sufficient technical resources, to the problems posed by conditions in South Africa.

Where urban African music, for instance, has responded to the challenges of the disintegrative tendencies of city life with an amazing suppleness and subtlety, black writing shows the cracks and tension of language working under severe strain. Where African music and dance have moved forward, not through renouncing tradition but by fusing diverse elements into an integrated whole, black fiction has renounced African tradition without showing itself capable of benefiting from the accumulated example of modern European literature. To put it bluntly: nothing stands behind the fiction of black South Africans – no tradition, whether indigenous, such as energizes *The Palm-Wine Drinkard* or alien such as is most significantly at work in the latest fiction by Camara Laye.

If black South African writers have read modern works of literature they seem to be totally unaware of their most compelling innovations; they blithely go on 'telling stories' or crudely attempting to solve the same problems which have been solved before – or if not solved, problems to which European practitioners, from Dostoevsky to Burroughs, have responded with greater subtlety, technical originality and sustained vigour; and black South Africans write, of course, as though Dostoevsky, Kafka or Joyce had never lived. Is it not possible without sounding either superior or unpatriotic, to ask how a fiction written by people conversant with the history of the development of modern fiction can reveal no awareness of the existence of *Notes From Underground, Ulysses* or such similar works? For make no mistake about this, it is not an instance of writers who have assimilated so well the lessons of the masters that they are able to conceal what they have learned; rather is it an example of a group of writers operating blindly in a vacuum.

This primitiveness or mere concern with *telling* the story may be supposed to have its own virtues. In contrast with Europe for instance, where it is impossible to write without being conscious of the fossilized examples of literary tradition, this lack of self-consciousness may seem a welcome liberation from the burden of tradition: it could even be supposed to allow for a certain freshness and originative power in the writing; yet these are virtues which would be very difficult to locate in fiction by black South Africans. We certainly have nothing to counterpose against the imaginative power of Chinua Achebe's *Things Fall Apart* or the placid grace of its style. Nor do we have anything to equal the teeming inventive genius of Amos Tutuola's *The Palm-Wine Drinkard*. To read a novel like Richard Rive's *Emergency* is to gain a minute glimpse into a literary situation which seems to me quite desperate. It may even be wondered whether it might not be more prudent to 'renounce literature temporarily', as some have advised, and solve the political problem first rather than continue to grind out hackneyed third-rate novels of which *Emergency* is a leading example.

What we do get from South Africa therefore – and what we get most frequently – is the journalistic fact parading outrageously as imaginative literature. We find here a type of fiction which exploits the ready-made plots of racial violence, social apartheid, interracial love affairs which are doomed from the beginning, without any attempt to transcend or transmute these given 'social facts' into artistically persuasive works of fiction. Thus a story like 'The Situation' by Bloke Modisane relies mainly on the 'inside' information about the exciting underground life of the Johannesburg township of which the author happens to be in possession; and through the limited power of the documentary technique we are taken on a tour of the Johannesburg *shebeen* we are offered glimpses of the motley company of thugs, pimps and their 'nice-time' girls; and we are made to feel the tension between rival gangs which is as gratuitous as the tension generated in a Western film by the presence of two fast draws in the same saloon; yet, even with the exploitation of the earthiest detail the story still flounders on a general lack of ideas; it collapses finally because both in its method and in its theme the story is a stereotype and the excitement is external – part and parcel of a dangerous social stratum – and does not come from the inner tension of creative talent confronting inept matter. At the end there is neither impact nor revelation but a kind of cessation. Yet without this power for so re-ordering experience, and for so transmuting the given social facts that we can detect an underlying moral imagination at work, it is difficult to see why we should give up the daily newspaper in favour of creative fiction, for the newspapers would tell us just as much about life.

In an interesting essay called 'The Function of Criticism' Mr Robert Langbaum ably states the case for creative literature; but in reading him I seemed to be reading a carefully inscribed charge-sheet against the kind of fiction I am talking about. Mr Langbaum writes;

> The imagination . . . remains for us, the faculty which accounts for literature as revelation, as a maker of values.

Quite obviously literature as 'revelation' or as a 'maker of values' is not likely to result from a type of writing which relies on the technique of *cinéma-vérité* – a technique which consists largely in training the camera long enough on the passing scene in the desperate hope that art may result by accident. It might very well be that the vitality of African writing in South Africa lies mainly in the area of non-fiction. Certainly the profile of the Sophiatown ghetto in Bloke Modisane's book, *Blame Me On History*, or Ezekiel Mphahlele's autobiographical essay, *Down Second Avenue*, are far superior to anything these writers have attempted in creative fiction.

Even the way Bloke Modisane structures the book shows a dedication to a superior form of realism which succeeds partly because the author is alive to the fact that reality itself is elusive to the process of Time as an orderly sequence of events. It seems to me a pity that Bloke Modisane has not exploited his potential talent for satire which he exhibited to advantage in his story, 'The Dignity of Begging':

> One of these days when I'm on my annual leave, I hope to write a book on begging, something like a treatise on the subject. It will be written with sensitivity and charm, brimful with sketches from life, and profusely illustrated with coloured photographs, with easy-to-follow rules on the noblest and oldest occupation in the world: Begging!

If Ezekiel Mphahlele has so far produced no profoundly moving work of fiction he differs from the other black South African writers in his pre-occupations which, in his most recent fiction, reveals how keenly aware Ezekiel Mphahele is of the intractable nature of South African experience when it has to be contained within an artistic form; and this intractability has something to do both with the over-melodramatic nature of the political situation and the barrenness and infertile nature of tradition. It has always amazed me that bad writers should consider racial conflict a God-sent theme when prudent writers know how resistant this theme has proved to be to any artistic purpose. This is not only true in Africa; American Negro fiction, with the exception of Jimmy Baldwin's *Go, Tell it On the Mountain* and Ralph Ellison's *The Invisible Man*, has proved incapable of revealing half the depth and richness of Negro life as expressed by American Negro music, especially the blues. The main hope for Ezekiel Mphahlele as a writer is that he is aware of all these things, and latterly he has been moving in the direction of saying something positive about black experience in South Africa instead of writing, as many of our writers do, as though everything the blacks did in the country was a reaction to white oppression.

He had already begun to do this, of course, in some of his stories based on quirky Newclare characters, though these stories were often little more than sketches; and of course his small volume of collected stories issued by Mbari Publications, in Nigeria under the title: *The Living & Dead* has some good examples of this type of fiction in 'The Suitcase' and 'He and the Cat'. However, it is in his most recent story published in the Johannesburg quarterly, *The Classic*, that Ezekiel Mphahlele has given the best accounting for his talent.

Now the most remarkable thing about Africans – this is not always to their benefit – is hardly their conservatism; on the contrary it is their ability to absorb alien influences and manners and to adapt them to their particular tradition. In a city like Johannesburg, for example, a study of the African languages as they are spoken today would reveal a great deal about this African willingness to borrow and to adapt foreign words and concepts, which are thereafter given a new dimension altogether. I am thinking of words like 'situation' which is a term of abuse for members of the African middle class trying to 'situate' themselves above the masses. And so is 'sitshuzimi' which is an adaptation of the phrase 'Excuse me', also used in a satirical vein to refer to pretentious half-baked Africans trying to ape the ways of white folk by a repetitious use of similar phrases.

So far as I have been able to gather from such evidence as I possess, what Ezekiel Mphahlele has been trying to do is reclaim some of these words from the African languages back into the English where they have their origin anyway; and simultaneously he exploits the new connotative element they have since acquired by their association with the African languages: in doing so he manages to give them a slightly ambivalent satirical content which they would otherwise not possess. Or he merely makes African idioms and speech rhythms stand behind his English, something which Nigerians do all the time. The re-arrangement of syntax, for instance, often achieves a comical effect similar to that arrived at by American Jewish writers, most notably, Bernard Malamud. For instance, Africans in South Africa seem unable to think of a government as a faceless bureaucratic institution; they always seek to personify it before they can properly conceive it. Thus in Ezekiel Mphahlele's story an old woman rebukes a policeman who is only too ready to hide behind the vast nameless authority of the government:

Is this how you would like your mother or your wife to be treated, I mean your own mother?

I am doing the government's work.

Go and tell that government of yours that he is full of dung to send you to do such things. Sies. Kgoboromente Kogoboromente! You and him can go to hell where you belong.

This is as close as you can get to the quality of African speech in English transposition, and the effect of course is always slightly comical.

In his story 'In Corner B' Ezekiel Mphahlele has gone further; he successfully exploits that vein of tragi-comedy which has been so fruitfully mined in African song and dance and in the rudimentary urban African theatre, but which has not, to my knowledge, been usefully tapped in African writing. By situating a number of episodes within the framework of an African funeral he also achieves a number of ironies. Firstly, he does this by juxtaposition; those who come to such funerals, still largely traditional, are often there to mourn as well as to enjoy a ceremony which is not without some festive gaiety. The juxtaposition is one between the African's very profound sense of piety in the face of Death as well as the well-known African tendency to turn sad religious occasions into moments, not of self-abnegation but of sensual expression whose orgiastic force and redemptive lust are anti-Puritanical in spirit, protracted as the traditional period of mourning is in these African funerals, they have become notorious occasions for exploiting the hospitality of the bereaved family. They have also become happy hunting grounds for sex-starved matrons and the iniquitous young, as well as helping to bring together numerous relatives from various parts of the country who use the funeral as an occasion for prosecuting familial matters. Thus during the mourning we see surreptitious groups of carousing drinkers – 'drowning de sorry'; there is a family quarrel between rival cousins of the dead man over the right of disposing the body; there is a copulation in the yard between a young couple who quietly rejoin the singing after the brief release of sexual tension, a need which is just as pressing, if not more, than the need to express grief.

'Shh!' The senior uncle of the dead man cut in to try to keep the peace. And he was firm. 'What do you want to turn this house into? There is a widow in there in grief and here you are you haven't got what the English call respection. Do you want all the people around to laugh at us, think little of us? All of us bury our quarrels when we come together to weep over a dear one who has left; what nawsons is this?'

In the past what had always put me off Ezekiel Mphahele's writing was a certain dullness of tone, much like the ponderous speech of a dull-witted person, so that it was often difficult to pursue the story to its ending.

The gems were often embedded in a thick mud of cliche and lustreless writing: a succession of simple clauses, for instance, linked together by semi-colons. The texture of the prose had the feel and look of sweaty labour much like the stains of honest sweat on the cloth-cap of the toiling proletariate; but hardly congenial for being honest. For instance, in order to expose the inner thoughts of his characters, Ezekiel would often reflect in this clumsy manner:

> Now she was ill. She was about to have a baby; a third baby. And with nothing to take home for the last two months, his savings running out, he felt something must be done. Not anything that would get him into jail. No, not that . . .

And so it would go on. Somewhere along the line the monologue of his hero becomes merged with that of the author. The danger with this kind of writing is that it can often become a substitute for action in the story or a substitute for a more ingenious solution to the problem of flashbacks. At his slowest it contributed to a considerable amount of dullness in Ezekiel Mphahlele's writing. Yet some of these problems of style were clearly attributable to external causes: the strain of maintaining an equilibrium in a dangerously melodramatic situation. If one went too far the other way in an effort to match with language the violence of the streets, the prose became strained, brittle and frayed; so that the flatness in Mphahlele's writing was sometimes due to an honourable attempt to remain 'cool under fire'. It seems to me that in the latest work Mphahlele's writing has become tighter, more solid and assured as he acquires a more properly synthesized vocabulary to deal with the stresses of South African life. He has achieved greater authority and better grip on his own particular idiom: the result is a happier fluency of tone.

Now to return to Richard Rive, about whose work I had some mean things to say earlier on: If one approaches his latest work, especially his novel, *Emergency*, with sorrow and despair, it is because of the promise his early fictional pieces like 'Rain' and 'WillieBoy' had aroused which seems largely to have remained unfulfilled in this novel.

'Are you for American poetry or for poetry?' was Ezra Pound's truculent question to Marianne Moore. We need only to transpose the names of the continents to put this question with some profit to our own African writers, not because the roots are unimportant but because literature is more important. And as a work of literature, Richard Rive's novel seems to me quite unfortunate. Its value can only be to add a footnote, and not a desperately needed one, to the political events leading to the declaration of a state of emergency in South Africa in 1960. The novel is wholly unimaginative, totally uninspired and exceedingly clumsy in construction. For instance, the gimmicky way in which he mentions various unrelated characters and what they are doing at some particular moment in time doesn't work; it remains purely *that*: a gimmick. If Rive borrowed the technique from James Joyce's *Ulysses* the result of this borrowing was unfortunate because *Emergency* lacks the imaginative force, the resonance, suggestiveness and energy of James Joyce's novel; it also lacks strong clear characters which provided a focus for the multiplicity of detail that made up Joyce's Dublin.

The main action of the story, as I said, takes place within the framework of political activity by left-wing and nationalist organizations which culminated in the Pan Africanist campaign of 1960 and the riots of Langa township and the shootings of Sharpeville. The central characters are Andrew Dreyer, a product of the Cape Coloured slum of District Six, someone whom we may presume to represent in some limited fashion the author's view of life, Abe Hanslo, from the better middle-class suburb of Walmer Estate and Ruth Talbot, a liberal white girl, all of whom are students when we meet them at the University of Cape Town. During their university career and later, we see these three and a supporting cast of other characters gradually sucked into the vortex of South African politics. By the end of the book the state of emergency has been declared and the trio is on the run, pursued by the Security Police; and it is Andrew Dreyer finally who makes the decision to stop running and to stay behind and face the consequences of his political activities.

Apart from bad jerky writing of which this novel has examples in great abundance and long chunks of dialogue which add nothing to the understanding of character, the novel fails dismally to set us ablaze with excitement, despite the melodramatic nature of the events, because none of the characters have any massive presence as people, Richard Rive's main weakness is his inability to create realizable people in the manner in which another Cape coloured writer, Alex la Guma, succeeds in a stroke. Right to the end of the novel all three main characters, to say nothing of the white ones, remain completely unrealized because Riva's use of dialogue is never to reveal his characters but to present argument about the political situation, which is his main interest. Thus the characters never use words which are uniquely theirs; but words and argument which suggest the position of the various ethnic or political groups they represent. While the situation is everything the characters are flat and uninteresting. In Rive's novel, as indeed in most of the stories recently published in *Quartet* by four Cape coloured writers, there are no real full-blooded characters with real blood to spill; no characters whose fighting or love-making has the stench of real living people: they are cardboard pieces and cardboard pieces don't spill any blood. Embarrassingly, what comes out of the apartheid machine when it has ground to a standstill is not human flesh but cardboard pulp.

To say all this is indirectly, to pay tribute to Alex la Guma, the Cape coloured writer whose novella, *A Walk in the Night*, has been published cheaply by Mbari Publications of Nigeria but a novella which most assuredly deserves wide notice abroad. Paradoxically, of all the black writers who have suffered the most in the hands of the South African Government, la Guma has been longest on the receiving end. He was one of the defendants in the protracted Treason Trial; he has been banned from attending gatherings of any kind and detained in prison several times. He is now under house arrest in Cape Town;[1] his writings cannot, of course, be published or quoted in the country. This means he has been virtually denied the right to earn a living, as he has always done, through journalism.

If Alex la Guma tills the same apartheid plot which the other writers have so exhaustively worked up, what distinguishes him as a true novelist is his enthusiasm for life as it is lived. He has the artist's eye for the interesting detail; his stories and novels are sagging under the weight of real people waging a bloody contest with the forces of oppression; and credibly they celebrate their few moments of victory in sex, cheap Cape wine and stupid fights. The rooms they inhabit smell of decay, urine and sweat; they share them with 'roaches, fleas, bugs, lice. Their only triumph is that they are human – superlatively human; and this is their sole claim upon our imagination.

Another quality of la Guma as a writer is the suggestive power of his prose. 'A Glass of Wine', for instance, is a superbly observed story with an appropriate dialogue that relies on the speech idioms of the Cape Malay folk. The boy who was 'tall and young and thin as a billiard cue' is really white though he comes to the shebeen to visit one of the coloured girls. As for the girl, instantly she comes to life before us as la Guma discreetly observes her: 'She did not look at the boy, but knew that he was there, and looking at him in turn I could see the deep flush of his own face and the gentle lowering of the eyelids as he watched her.' There is marvellous irony here which is beautifully sustained, when one of the drunks, unaware that the boy is really white, gently mocks the young couple: 'With such love, blushing and all, these two must mos marry.'

At the end of the story there is revelation, not only of the tragedy of the young lovers who cannot marry, but of the absurdity of life itself.

'You and your wedding,' I told him as we went up the street. 'You know that white boy can't marry the girl, even though he may love her. It isn't allowed.'

'Jesus,' Arthur said in the dark. 'Jesus. What the hell.'

---

[1] He was eventually able to leave the country in 1966, and now lives in exile in London.

In *A Walk in the Night* la Guma follows the progress of Michael Adonis, a coloured boy thrown out of his factory job for talking back to the white foreman; and a supporting cast of thugs, derelicts, spivs, neurotic cops 'doomed for a certain term to walk the night'. By the end of this night Adonis has killed under an impulse a harmless old man; a neurotic police-man has shot a small-time thug; a penniless man has been 'rolled' for money; but incontestably life has also been celebrated in the cheap bars, speakeasies and wretched slumhouses along the Harlem-like ghetto of Cape Town's District Six. This impressive short work has distinct Dostoevskian undertones, which, I hope, is not too large a claim to make for it. It is inexcusable that European and American publishers who are in such indecent haste to put into print any mediocre talent from Africa have ignored this novel.

There are a few other black South African writers like Arthur Maimane, Casey Motsisi, Dugmore Boetie,[2] Harry Mashabela, Can Themba,[2] whom I have not mentioned at length, though some of them write much abler prose than many writers on the continent. This is because the work of these writers has been largely in the area of non-fiction or because they have produced only one or two short stories upon which it is impossible to make an estimation of their talent. Of these Can Themba has perhaps the liveliest mind and the best command of the English language; but apart from his recent story published in *Modern Stories From Africa* he has been annoyingly shiftless, throwing off cheap pot-holders when magazines demanded them. Casey Motsisi is perhaps our wiliest satirical talent in South Africa but his success has been in the area of sketches so far which owe a great deal in inspiration to Langston Hughes' '*Simple Speaks His Mind*.' I have seen only one story by Dugmore Boetie which was extra-ordinarily witty, powerful and ironical, if also brutal; one would like to see more writing by him. It also had the tough pitiless nerve which one has come to associate with the sensibility of modern literature.

---

[2] Both now dead. Dugmore Boetie's autobiographical novel *Familiarity is the Kingdom of the Lost* written with Barney Simon was published posthumously in 1970.

Lewis Nkosi
and David Rubadiri

▼▼▼▼▼▼▼▼▼▼▼▼▼▼▼▼▼▼▼▼▼▼▼▼▼▼▼▼▼▼▼▼

Relating Literature and Life

[1966]

THIS is the last of the National Educational Television series, *African Writers of Today*, which *Negro Digest* has published in full with the permission of NET. The first, 'The Black Writer in Exile', appeared in the December 1964 issue; the second, 'Black Writers, White Readers', appeared in the March 1965 issue; the third, 'The Literary Impact of Negritude', was published in the May 1965 issue; the fourth, 'The Problems of African Culture and Literature', appeared in the June 1965 issue; and the fifth, 'The African Writer in Search of His Audience', was in the November 1965 issue. This, the sixth and final presentation, is an interview with David Rubadiri, the poet and educator, at his residence at Soche Hill College in Nyasaland. Mr Rubadiri is interviewed by Lewis Nkosi, the self-exiled South African journalist who hosted the NET series, and Joseph Kariuki, a poet and educator from Kenya.

NKOSI: Now, Dave, the first question I would like to ask you has very much to do with your personal drive as an educationist in Nyasaland. I would like to find out from you just what makes you run so hard . . . 'What Makes Sammy Run,' so to speak.

RUBADIRI: Well nothing really, I think it's a majority interest in my own profession and, secondly, one feels that in Africa, here maybe our answer lies in the educational field and that gives one a tremendous kick in doing things, because one knows that he is going somewhere, albeit slowly; but fairly fast.

NKOSI: Well, there's certainly lots of young people who feel this about the continent and they aren't as active as you are. There must be some kind of urge that makes you want to do this.

RUBADIRI: I don't think so. I think you're being unfair to these young men actually. I mean, look at Joe, for instance, he's been a schoolmaster for a great part of his life, although he's branched into business now. I think he's very much an educationist at heart. And I think at this present stage, in Africa, whatever little one does in any one field, one tends to do it with a new sense of dedication, a new gusto and spring of enthusiasm just comes out of everything one does.

KARIUKI: David, perhaps it might be interesting for us to know something of your background, something of the forces which have influenced you not only recently, but also in your formative years.

RUBADIRI: Yes, well the natural forces ... family background, parents, friends and the schools one goes to. I think my school has been a major influence in my development.

KARIUKI: Which was this?

RUBADIRI: This was a school in Uganda called King's College.

NKOSI: It seems to me that this great movement of Africans throughout the continent, say, Nigerians coming to Nyasaland and you being sent to school in Uganda, that this isn't something that used to take place on a great scale, about ten years ago, at the time you were growing up. Was this something normal or was it rare?

RUBADIRI: No, not quite normal. It's quite a new thing in fact. I think there are two reasons why there is an interchange of African people between the territories now. The first one is that new emerging countries in Africa need new manpower which is specialized. Say, for instance, we've got a team of Nigerian lawyers here. We haven't got enough lawyers in Nyasaland. They will be able to understand the people they are dealing with, the conditions which they have to meet here, and maybe their influence will be more lasting than if we imported a lot of lawyers from other countries.

NKOSI: Well, the other question I would like to put to you has something to do with the conflict that we hear so much about between the Western way of life and the traditional African way of life. I would like to know whether you have experienced this, and to what extent, and how you have resolved it. But I don't want to ask this question directly. I'd like to show you one of the poems that you've written and can you just read it over to us.

RUBADIRI: Yes.

NKOSI: And then tell us what emotions you were experiencing when you were writing the poem.

RUBADIRI: Yes. I wrote this poem as a student at Makerere College.

NKOSI: Yes.

RUBADIRI: ... At a time, I think, when my own emotional and intellectual conflict was being shaped and had come into contact with new and rather powerful ideas in the subject I was studying at the University ... I'll read it through as you request.

NKOSI: Okay.

RUBADIRI: And then perhaps we might be able to talk more about it.

The Tide That From The West Washes Africa To The Bones

> The tide that from the West
> washes Africa to the bones gargles
> through my ribs and gathers the bones,
> clustering rough and polished.
> to fling them back destitute
> to the river bank.
>
> The tide that from the
> West washes the soul of Africa,
> Washes the buoys of its spirit and
> tears the moorings
> apart, till blood red the tide
> becomes and heartsick
> the wound. The tide that from the
> West washes Africa,
> Once washed a wooden cross.

NKOSI: What was happening when you were writing that?

RUBADIRI: Well, frankly, I don't think I can tell you in any sort of lucid terms. But I think, basically, here you have a personal conflict; first, with Christianity and the values that Christianity stands for and, second, with a Christianity which was established as a government power; third, with a way of life whose values have not been questioned by me before, but which now, in the light of new ideas clouding in my mind, have begun to suddenly spring out. It is like a bursting out of a smoke screen and coming face to face with a new visitor, a new view where one didn't know where to stretch a hand to clutch on.

KARIUKI: Do you find that you get disinterested, perhaps, when some of these conflicts are getting resolved?

RUBADIRI: Sometimes, yes – most times, no. I think you'll agree, Joe, that for quite a number of us who have in many parts grown up, grown up not in the African traditional village, but have been uprooted as youngsters and grown up in missions and gone to mission schools and have come face to face with the power that the white man yielded as a governor, have had to come to a time when you feel you've got to feel the ground under your feet and try to start growing roots, as it were, to reach towards something which will nourish what one is keeping in the head. And perhaps this is an indication of that desire, to try and reground one's self.

KARIUKI: Will this suggest that your poetry will reveal these problems and conflicts as you go on or do you think you're developing towards a quieter, more settled state?

RUBADIRI: I don't know. The things which are interesting me now, with my country getting independence and, therefore into nationhood, are resolving quite a number of these personal problems, because my major interests at the moment are trying to play the little part I can in contributing towards the reconstruction of my country. I feel I'm a human being. I'm a man now, and these personal conflicts, which went beyond the personal and covered other aspects of my life, which have now been resolved, are being reduced. And so I begin to write more like . . . like myself as an African who's got roots or beginning to get them, as opposed to the young student who had to live between two worlds, as it were, two values of life.

KARIUKI: Talking about the development of your own country in Africa today, we have been much more concerned with economic problems and social problems, problems of poverty and problems of health, as President Nyerere quite often mentions. Do you think that poetry, and literature, generally, is a luxury perhaps; that perhaps we can't afford poets and writers and we should concern ourselves with the daily living kind of thing, or do you feel that the poet has a place in the new Africa that we are trying to shape for the future?

RUBADIRI: I think any creative person or any creative spirit in Africa today has not only got a place but can never be regarded as a luxury; I think the only thing that Africa has got to boast about, and one which I think can contribute towards humanity, is the spiritual force which we still retain. We haven't, speaking with the background of my own country for instance . . . a rough road doesn't bother me very much. The fact that when I take people to my capital city I can't point at skyscrapers or fantastic machinery doesn't bother me at all. Sometimes I'm thankful about this. And I feel that, very much at heart, the African is not only a poet, but is a creative human being. He still has senses of values which, I think, a number of our friends in the other countries are beginning to lose very fast because of fast and rapid economic development. Of course, I want these things to come. I want a better way of life for my people, but it must be directed with a spiritual force behind it, not just for show.

NKOSI: Yes, David, before I ask you the next question I would like to know, in your relationship with African politicians in your country, do you find that they are sensitive to this need for poets to play a part in the development of your cultures or of the cultures of all, or do they think poets are disturbers of the peace?

RUBADIRI: No, I don't think there's any animosity towards people who grow long hair and pretend to write poetry or anything like that. In fact, our own Prime Minister, Dr Banda, you will notice, has chosen for his cabinet for his country a number of very young men between the ages of thirty and thirty-five. Three-quarters of them have been schoolmasters; one of them, the Minister of Education, himself, once wrote a novel in the vernacular and he set up a committee to encourage writing, both vernacular and in English. And in our own party newspaper, there's a special page which is devoted mainly to people who contribute verse to it. And the new committee which is going to organize our museum has been given specific instruction to try and build up its fund of local, creative works of art.

NKOSI: Yes, I think we ought to move, perhaps, to the tradition that we hear so much about. Time and time again, African writers are exhorted to use the African tradition. They are asked to reactivate it and to employ it in the works that they are writing today. Just to what extent can, say, a modern African poet use the African traditions, and is this necessary – especially for an African poet using a metropolitan language? Just how do you see this question of tradition?

RUBADIRI: I think we've got to accept that the new form we are using at the moment, the technical part of it, is basically a foreign one, is basically European. We are writing verse which, technically, is very much influenced by European poets, for instance. But speaking of the personal level, one cannot break away from things which nourish one's way of life. I think you know that our strongest point in literary forms is the oral tradition, and most of us have passed through this oral tradition from our parents and our friends as youngsters. Now, when I sit down to write, I don't consciously make an effort to try and be an African writer by trying to adapt some so-called African forms. The echoes of the African tradition come to me subconsciously, I hear them, and perhaps this is the only African part – or influence – that I can confess of; otherwise, I think the technical part of it is entirely conditioned by my experience with reading European literature.

KARIUKI: Talking about traditions, David, I'd like to know what you feel about the forms which are being used today by writers in England. Because, although we have learned English and its own tradition and the Englishman writing today is using a tradition which has very extensive roots, and we are still foreigners to their literature and, also, the forces which motivate the writer are the result let's say of the last fifty years in Europe, it's all very European centered. Now, we are a young country, a country with hopes and so on, looking forward, as it were, to the future. Do you feel that we should try and develop our own forms, although we are using English, or do you think that somehow we can be fitted into the mainstream of the English traditions?

RUBADIRI: I think this is the exciting part of it. I don't think we can control the forms which are going to emerge; I don't think we can condition what is going to come out of African writing in our age or time. I think this is a thing which we've got to wait and watch and see how it's going to take place, for instance. I think, in the next twenty to twenty-five years time, we will begin to feel that African writers, in fact, are contributing a new form altogether in verse writing, or in drama writing, or even in novel writing. We begin to see it, for instance, in Achebe. We're beginning to see it in some of the poets who have been publishing for a long time. But I feel very indignant to try and begin to write critical works suggesting that the African writers should start developing their own form. I don't think even European literature, which has influenced us, is really foreign. Most great works of art, I think, have got this universal appeal. That's a generalization, I know, but let's not tie up these chaps; the most important thing is to let them write.

KARIUKI: Trying to follow-up on that . . . I'm not thinking so much of our writers being tied down to, you know, certain traditions which are African. I'm thinking of our writers being tied down by European traditions, and finding themselves trying to use forms, maybe, which are the result of a development which may not be entirely relevant in our country.

RUBADIRI: Well, what would you suggest, Joe?

NKOSI: Well, what T. S. Eliot calls – the dissociation of feeling and so on . . . the whole pessimism . . . is Beckett really relevant to Africa at the moment?

RUBADIRI: Is Beckett relevant to Africa at the moment?

NKOSI: Yes, this problem about communication: you can't communicate with somebody and you use the whole stage to show human beings who are trapped in those situations, and they simply can't get to each other. Is this the problem we are going to concern ourselves with when we are in a revolutionary situation?

RUBADIRI: Yes. I think I see your point now. No, of course not. And I'd hate to see many of our dramatists begin to put their plays in picture frames as you say. I think we've got a very, very strong dramatic tradition in our own way of life. I think you've just got to go into a village and see drama in action without any producer behind it all and I think it is the outdoor theatre that's going to be the great thing in African drama as it develops. It's a thing which I don't think one can, consciously, really control or direct. Each writer is going to find himself into knots at one moment or other and then hit out to find new forms.

NKOSI: Yes. Dave, we're running out of time, I'm afraid, but I'd like to ask you another question and this question concerns the teaching of African literature in schools. I know that you were a delegate to one of the conferences very much concerned with this problem – the fact that up to now, African literature has not been taught in African schools. But what I'm interested in is, how is this literature going to be selected and what are the standards going to be used and who is going to select it? And also, whether you feel that there might be a danger that teachers, anxious to use African literature, might tend to invent African literature where it doesn't exist really?

RUBADIRI: Yes. This is a risk which I think all of us have got to take. For instance, in January, here, I'm going to open a new day secondary school and have been given permission to experiment in drawing up the syllabus. As you know, we've been tied down by overseas exams for a long time and that didn't give a chance for anyone to experiment. Books are expensive. Whatever book you buy is going to cost a lot of money in a country which is as poor as ours at the moment. And so I think the whole matter of beginning to introduce African literature in schools will largely depend on the individual teachers, whether they be African or European, who'll be given the duty of teaching literature to our children in the schools. Here at the college, I haven't got the money, for instance, to buy even thirty copies of Gerald Moore's anthology in Penguin . . . nor can I get Langston Hughes' book. And so I mainly use duplicated sheets and I hope by the end of the term we shall have collected together a small little anthology which my teachers are going to take out with them when they go out to teach and maybe use some of the poems which are mainly by African writers. As regards standards, that is a very tricky question because we haven't yet organized really, standard set, as it were. African works haven't been well discussed, they haven't been very widely discussed by scholars or critics and so on. And so, one must depend on one's judgement. Now, I think, to me, even a bad African poem is a useful thing to start from because when you are students you are starting from common ground; then you can branch-off to some of the more classic works and then, with that, one can begin to establish standards of judgement and appreciation so that anybody can pick up a poem and be able to enjoy it, as well as say why he thinks it's good or bad; which I think is the essence of teaching literature – not to teach them poems, as such, but to teach them the tools of judgement.

NKOSI: Well, gentlemen, I think we're running short of time. I would have liked to ask you another question. We have been talking to David

Rubadiri, a poet and an educationist about whom you are likely to hear a lot as Nyasaland consolidates her independence. Dave is not only a firm believer in African nationalism, but he is also one of those rare African young men who now wish to see Africa conducting her affairs with tolerance and sophistication. ... Now, Dave, I thought that we could perhaps end this programme by showing some of the scenes we recorded earlier today when you lectured to your senior English students and read a poem by Roy Campbell.

RUBADIRI: Here you have a man who basically is an African because he's been born in Africa, he knows no other home. He's a European ... his home background, his main sense of values have been shaped by a European tradition. And yet, he cares about Africa. This country means something to him. As a child, he might have played with young African children out in the fields, in the gardens. They might have been chasing goats together. Every morning they might have gone to school, but the African child went to a bush school and Roy Campbell went to a European school. In the evening they met and played together like two great friends. Roy Campbell here is writing his poem on a Zulu woman, because, within the face of African womanhood, I think we begin to see the meaning of many of the values which we stand for, which will live. An African child is very much a product of its mother, and within African motherhood, Roy Campbell brings out his own personal conflicts as an African and also as a European who has been bred and brought up in Africa. And so I'll read the Roy Campbell poem to you ...

> When in the sun the hot red acres smoulder,
>   down where the sweating gang its labour
> plies, a girl flings down her hoe, and from
>   her shoulder unslings her child, tormented
> by the flies.
>
> She takes him to a ring of shadow pooled by
>   thorn trees: purple with the blood of
> ticks, while her sharp nails, in slow caresses
>   ruled, prowl through his hair with sharp
> electric clicks;
>
> His sleepy mouth, plugged by the heavy nipple,
>   tugs like a puppy, grunting as he feeds:
> Through his frail nerves her own deep langours
>   ripple like a broad river sighing through
> its reeds.

Yet in that drowsy stream his flesh imbibes
   an old unquenched unsmotherable heat –
the curbed ferocity of beating tribes, the
   sullen dignity of their defeat.

Her body looms above him like a hill within
   whose shades a village lies at rest.
Or the first cloud so terrible and still that
   bears the coming harvest in its breast.

Okello Oculi

▼▼▼▼▼▼▼▼▼▼▼▼▼▼▼▼▼▼▼▼▼▼▼▼▼▼▼▼▼▼

Interview

THE following excerpts are from an interview with Mr Oculi by Marti Mueller[1] and Laura Tanna[1] which took place on November 3, 1970 in Kampala, Uganda.

MARTI: Why did you turn to writing as a form of expression?

OKELLO: I didn't turn to it. I just started it.

MARTI: Was there something that motivated or attracted you?

OKELLO: At a time in '67 there was what you could call a school of thought really. You must remember that at this time the West Africans wrote earlier than the East Africans did. Who was there . . . Wole Soyinka, Achebe, Okigbo. We didn't hear very much about South African writers. The trouble was the way they were presented. Remember that, especially the West African authors, were published by Heinemann, which is a British publishing house, and we were given the impression at Makerere that the only literature which was going to sell was the kind that would please this foreign, British firm; not literature that would be tied up with African sentiments and African needs . . . I wasn't with the literature department but I was working with some of my friends on *The Makererean* . . . I used to hear some of their complaints. They were budding writers. . . . So I wrote and I must say at the time, the first nonsense I wrote was immediately after *Song of Lawino* by Okot. *Song of Lawino* touched exactly that nerve which we had been arguing. The response of Kampala was so spontaneous that we thought we were on the right side.

LAURA: You said this was in '67?

OKELLO: '67.

LAURA: Were you doing any writing when you were in California?

OKELLO: No. The only writing I did in California was a letter to the

---

[1] Marti Mueller is an American freelance journalist currently working in Africa. Laura Tanna is an American graduate student in the Department of African Languages and Literature at the University of Wisconsin and a resident of Uganda.

Stanford student newspaper which was severely cut when I said that people like Livingstone and Speke didn't discover the Nile. There had been people living there all the time who had seen the Nile and all those mountains before. The Editors at Stanford didn't like that at all. That was the only writing I did.

MARTI: Were you influenced very much in your writing by Okot?

OKELLO: I would say so. He confirmed this yearning we had for self-assertion, not only self in terms of ourselves, but self in the collective sense, what we felt was the African sense of assertion. Lawino was written as a translation from the Luo version and it was translated in such a way that the English language was twisted to serve the purposes of Acoli ways of thinking. And me, speaking a language which is very close to Acoli, as I read *Song of Lawino*, although reading it in English, I was reading it in Luo.

LAURA: It's really that close to the original?

OKELLO: Oh yes.

MARTI: In terms of your own poetry, is most of it written in English?

OKELLO: First of all I don't know if it's poetry yet. I can't decide if it's poetry or not. I don't know what poetry is. I think they're shortlegged sentences; an irresponsible way of writing in which one doesn't spell out fully what one feels. I don't know how the African is supposed to split in two once he's learnt English. Half of his mind is supposed to be written in English and half of his mind is supposed to be written in his own language. There is no other half left for some other language.

LAURA: Then when you write do you translate in your mind from Lango into English?

OKELLO: I don't really know which comes first, writing a certain way to get a certain effect or just writing, feeling, recording an idea. The third category is starting off with thinking independent of language. I think you're making the statement that one has to think in language form.

LAURA: No, one can think in images.

OKELLO: If one can think in images that seems to fit into my category of thinking both independent of language and of an audience. I think there is that category.

LAURA: Phrases like 'earlinesses helplessness' or 'screams of goodbye unintended' – this way of twisting language – how much of this do you attribute to you and the images you're trying to get out, and how much is because of your Lango language?

OKELLO: I really don't know how one can isolate these things. . . .

MARTI: How do you explain the fact that you and other writers at Makerere have escaped the Western style of thinking when the tendency has been for years to imitate Shakespeare, say.

OKELLO: When you say tendency there is an implication of choice. When you say tendency that may be wrong. I suspect there was a lot of force used by the educational apparatus. Whoever was in charge of the people's education was insisting that we had to learn Shakespeare. We had no choice. We had to pass exams and the exams were about Shakespeare, in the language of Shakespeare's mother tongue. And I think in situations where one has to pass an exam one has to get good marks . . .

We may be unnecessarily harsh on some of the writers who were older than we were, who grew up in the colonial period and who were trying to express themselves within a context that was very rigid and rough. We grew up free. I grew up in the first independence period – not to say that the British presence wasn't in all sorts of sneaky corners and camouflaged instead of being vulgar and open and very arrogant – so we had the chance of being ourselves. We had the chance of making a choice. I think most people who would have wanted to make a choice wouldn't have had what they wrote published in the first place, let alone to have the guts to tell anyone that they could be published. It would sound like if a little dog walked over to you and said 'You know I've got a manuscript. Would you like to look at it?' You might jump. This is the kind of pressure that they were up against.

MARTI: Can you comment on the style that recent expressions have taken.

OKELLO: *Song of Lawino* is written to touch the African nerve. There's really no other work that has succeeded in touching the African nerve as has *Song of Lawino*. A lot of these authors, like Joseph Buruga, a botanist here at Makerere who has written *The Abandoned Hut*, have been accused of being followers of Okot. I don't think this is a bad thing. All that Joseph Buruga seems to be saying is that Okot hit exactly on the kind of nerve, at the tissue, of the system. I don't think people should blame him for being what Okot was telling people. As for my nonsense, I think I was conscious, I had time to think about writing in such a way that it would be in tune with the way African women wanted to be told what they should be told. . . .

Okot was accused of crying for the simple, routine, boring, unsophisticated, primitive, savage culture of yesterday – if not yesterday, of the village, the life of the people. And Okot was depicted as somebody completely ungrateful to all the civilizing energies – the missionary, the gold mining prospector, the copper mining prospector, the business man and so on and so forth – had put into Okot's environment . . . the accusation was that ultimately what Okot was saying is that the African mind is so simple, so underdeveloped, that even with all these intrusions into his environment, all this effort – so many missionary sisters died in this country, so many businessmen died of malaria looking for wealth –

even after all that and all the people who taught Okot, they were never able to break through into his mind, into his brain, for him to be able to move away from the crying for the simplicity of the village. And they said, 'Well Okot is not writing poetry. It's too simple. Look at the sentences. Look at the words he's using. Look at the rhythm. It's too simple.' They almost said it was too lyrical but then that would have embarrassed them because in the history of European literature there is a tradition that's lyrical. So they just said it was too simple. So me, I said 'all right'. There may be a point in being a disciple of Okot. . . . So that in that sense I think we were responding to various factors. We were responding to intrusions into our environment. We were responding to the needs of our people – their political and social aspirations. We were responding to their cultural outrage.

LAURA: You said you call yourself a disciple of Okot. He's been characterized as a man who writes about politics, about religion, various things. You sort of weave them all together. There are passages that are completely original which Okot doesn't touch on, but then there are also passages that look as if they are direct inspirations from *Song of Lawino*. Is that right? You write about dance. You write about the priests. . . .

OKELLO: There's a very dangerous point here where one can be very dishonest in thinking. I think that for people like me, who are fairly dense, it's quite possible to read something and then it ferments in the head and when you write you don't realize that you've been influenced, that actually this man has made an impact on you. At the time that you are writing you think this idea is original. The idea may be original. It may have had an impact upon you because you already potentially had an idea on the same lines but then you don't know that he sharpened, he gave a sense of focus, to your sentiments. And then you find that you even have to use the same kind of language as he does. You're not really copying. You think it is your own language, your own song, whereas in fact it is the meeting between your own self-conscience and the message, the communication you took in from this fellow. When the two meet, they embrace each other and you pour out this anger.

LAURA: You both come from similar areas, I should think there would be some traditions that would be quite similar.

OKELLO: I think so . . . I found that some of the feelings and impact of my environment did certainly influence me. But as for the sense of being a disciple of Okot, we have been told over and over again to be a disciple of Shakespeare or people like D. H. Lawrence, Tennyson, Pope, and so on. For me at the time my argument was: 'why can't I be a disciple of Okot?' I'm not going to have any sense of apology about writing, especially in the way Okot wrote, in verse form and having one character singing all the way. I decided that I might as well be an interesting disciple in the sense of adding something new, hence the structure of *Orphan* with so many characters running around looking at this one character. But they all talk in verse, that much I wanted to be loyal to Okot – have it all in verse and long.

LAURA: Why did you call it a village opera?

OKELLO: Because I thought it was.

LAURA: In the introduction you make a point of saying that you're going to use African symbols. You say 'many of the symbols and figures used will be strange to some readers'. Frankly I didn't think there were that many strange symbols. There were a few, but did you put that in just as a form of protest to show that you were going to use African symbols and were proud of it?

OKELLO: You see there was a bit of juvenile arrogance in those lines in the preface. I was essentially being rude to the people I was arguing with. . . .

LAURA: Why did you use your own name?

OKELLO: At the time I had it all worked out. My argument then was – there were two arguments really – why should one tax somebody else's name? Because, in the Western novels anyway, somebody always finds somebody else's name to give you the problem, even if the problem is their own. Even in some very autobiographical pieces they always use somebody else's name. I thought this was a bit unfair considering that the other person is not going to write. And then of course my own name, which I'll not explain, has got a significance in one of the chapters. It was a Lango meaning of the name which was easy to fit in, which was in fact explained in the particular passage when the old man says 'Come you are one of us' and gives the meaning of Okello's name. Do you want me to go further?

LAURA: I wondered how much the effect of your book, especially with all of the emphasis upon isolation and loneliness, is the effect of your Western education? Could you have stayed here in Uganda and written the same thing or does the fact that you were overseas and probably experienced a certain degree of isolation intensify this feeling? How Western is the book?

OKELLO: I think it's Western in the sense that the language is Western. Perhaps the language has an influence which I haven't decided yet.

LAURA: But the idea itself of isolation – would someone who had never left the village feel this intense loneliness and isolation?

OKELLO: You see the idea of isolation shouldn't be taken out of context. I think isolation has to be seen in the context of the book itself. It has to be seen in the context of the way Africans think . . . but I'm generalizing very crudely. You know if you look at some of our culture, a lot of it is an attempt to make people feel that this isolation is not there, to tell people that this isolation is dangerous. It can be very dangerous to society because it is at the core of society. . . . As I say, even twins get born differently and somehow there is no way a person cannot die. I can only say that when a friend of mine dies, I always come back to this problem. When he dies, I put him in the grave and there's just nothing I can do about it. It's not me who has died. If he's wounded and he's shot and bleeding, he's really bleeding. I can only say 'I'm sorry' or some such crude thing. Society attempts to break this. There are ways to break this such as the idea of love, or the idea of clanship. These are an attempt to create an ideology that tries to get hold of this isolation and contain it.

It would appear that in Western thinking, isolation has been given a meaning, an impetus, a dynamic, that is really very dangerous, which has produced a whole way of organizing society. People are baptized in it in all sorts of ways: in *laisser faire*, in capitalism, in regionalism, what have you. But it seems to me that the West allowed isolation to take this victory, attached certain positive values to it: success, wealth, control over people. I think – I don't think – I know that the other side of isolation is, at one level, isolation is to be seen in relation to the title, *Orphan*.

How many people are orphans in Africa? Lots of people are orphans. Take a country like Kenya. Yesterday somebody was born in a village in contact with a certain soil, a certain kind of vegetation – the country-side. And for generations he's taught that man has tried to live in relation to this nature in order to make a living. There's a link between man and that nature. Then suddenly somebody comes and says 'You have to get out of here'. If nature is given the mother image – earth is given the mother image – and the white settler comes and the white settler says, 'Get out, we are now going to farm this land. We are now going to turn it into an agriculturally productive area, mechanize.' The triumph of isolation in that settler breeds an orphan. He's now Kikuyu. He's going to become a beggar in Nairobi. Then politically there are, oh God, there are people who recently were part of their society. That society took them into account. They had a skill in the society. They had milk, if they were women, they had milk which the society needed for generating, for bringing up the children into members of the society. They had the tenderness which the men didn't for keeping them going. They were participants in the history of that society. And then suddenly, colonialism comes. They are not supposed to be participants in the key decision-making of that society. They are no longer participants, and they turn into all sorts of strange creatures, distorted, brutalized. And tomorrow, comes independence and independence doesn't come to them. They are not participants in decision-making in that society . . . I think people are kept out because somebody else says, 'They're not part of me. I am alone. I am isolated from the peasant. I am educated and have wealth. I am more intelligent. . . .'

LAURA: There's a passage where you switch from an attack on colonialism into an attack on some of the neo-colonialism which you've just been talking about and I couldn't help but wonder . . . I mean I know how much you support the government[2] here and I wonder how you got away with writing such a strong attack. There are about two pages which are really very critical.

OKELLO: I don't know if I support the government here. I don't know if that's an accurate statement. . . . I don't think that I'm nationalistic in the sense of association with one government. I think really there's a way in which one begins to see nationalism not so much in support of a certain government but as a matter of life and death. After all, what is colonialism except a threat by one group of people to the lives of another group of people, ultimately. It would appear to me that when one is concerned with the lives of another group of people, one has to adopt a position of defending the lives of those people who are threatened. Of course it is a beautiful situation if the people in government have the same vision that ultimately what we're up to is making sure that these groups of people will also have a place in the sun, as in the dedication of *Orphan*. These people deserve a place in the sun. I think this requires a government that is concerned about the sort of transmutation.

MARTI: How do you deal with the role of the artist in society? What about the political implications? Should the artist feel conscious of bringing about change which can be seen in real terms? Or is it enough to inspire and accelerate things?

OKELLO: I don't know. . . . Somebody for generations worked to maintain that society that gave the artist birth. I think his first allegiance, his first sense of responsibility, is to that society, to play his own part. That's his gratitude. And secondly it would appear that even when he's born, that society allows him to breathe. Now they could bump him off any time they didn't want him around. It would appear to me that the link between the artist and society – it's primordial. It is so biological that I do not see the artist suddenly jumping up and looking at himself as some-body who is somebody who is somehow aloof from the problems of a particular society. Now the artist – the so-called artist – has got a responsibility of his own. He's an individual ultimately. Sometimes

---

[2] At the time of this interview the government in reference was that of Dr Milton Obote.

people talk about class and classes are a way of taking away individual responsibility. You are part of a collectivity. I think one cannot abdicate. If one is Christian, if one believes even for a moment that there is going to be a resurrection and a day of judgement, it would appear each one of us must answer for what part one played in our society. A character who poses as an artist is very easy to bribe. People interview him with tape recorders to play on his ego. . . . People sell the nonsense he writes. We give him a bank account and sooner or later, if you're not careful, you're going to find that society has worked a cobweb around him. And this individual responsibility I'm talking about is eroded.

I think it's very presumptuous to assume that an artist would create a revolution in society. It's very presumptuous. But perhaps there are some well-written things which have made people angry. It can also be argued the other way around, that the artist is an enemy of the people. In the situation where people are working vis-à-vis enemies, this so-called artist is likely to tell the other side the very things that shouldn't be told about his own people. And the other side is going to listen very carefully, interview him, and work out tricks that work exactly against the interests of that society. It would appear to me that looking at the English press, their book reviews, it is fantastic. When some character writes something explosive, they are the first people to absorb it, not the people about whom he's crying. The people who write the book reviews, on the B.B.C. are the people who know that he's dangerous. The very people he's crying for don't even get to the bookshop. They can't afford the bloody books, right?

LAURA: You just said that you don't see how the artist could really create a revolution. You once said that you wrote *Orphan* thinking of the African countries that are not yet liberated and that these are the orphans of Africa which the independent countries of Africa have now forgotten about and have left crying out in the cold. If you had that in mind when you wrote *Orphan*, were you just hoping to re-awaken the consciences of the independent countries?

OKELLO: Yeah, you know it's quite possible. . . .

LAURA: You said that one of the ways in which *Orphan* was not successful is the fact that it really isn't very obvious – the political implications aren't that obvious. Do you regret now that you didn't make it more obvious?

OKELLO: Well, I think so. I think that I'm a bit tired that *Orphan* is very . . . that people personalize *Orphan*. They look at it as an orphan boy and the connections that are supposed to be worked out are not there, not very clearly anyway. There was only one reviewer, somebody who works in the Ministry of Finance in the Uganda government who reviewed it once when it first came out and he wrote about the political implications of it. Since then most people have been talking all sorts of nonsense.

MARTI: I was going to ask how you juxtapose *Prostitute* with *Orphan*. Would *Prostitute* be an extension of *Orphan*?

OKELLO: You could say in a sense that *Orphan* was a village poem and *Prostitute* was an urban – what – novel, I suppose. Anyway, *Prostitute* is urban in its setting. . . . It is quite possible that the villager who was made an orphan by colonialism, who was made an orphan by politicians who set out in the post-independence period . . . this villager stands for an orphan. Perhaps the politicians who surround stand for prostitutes. Perhaps too, when the very idea of this history in which each one is supposed to participate clears away and one can remember and use the history itself which we cannot prostitute, then the continent can be seen under colonialism and under neo-colonialism as a prostitute raped. . . . See the orphan is not somebody who gives up. He's somebody who decides to fight and to assert himself. The prostitute ends up the last lines, something to the effect, 'If I die, do me a favour, please don't notice it.' Again, a bit of my juvenile arrogance. There's a kind of arrogance in that statement. And the prostitute, all through, she collapses only in relation to the village, which is her roots, which is her self. Face to face with her real self, she collapses. But face to face with all her friends in town, she's very tough. Maybe in that perspective there is still hope that she'll win in the end. After all, we don't know why they are prostitutes, or where they put their money. Maybe they use it for buying arms.

MARTI: Where do you go from here?

LAURA: You have a book of poems coming out, no?

OKELLO: Yes, the publisher is very interested. I've been trying to write something else. I think I'm trying to adopt a more explicitly fundamental perspective. I think both *Orphan* and *Prostitute* – although they are meant to apply throughout the continent in all sorts of ways – they're not very explicit. This one is perhaps a more explicit attempt to cover all Africa, which is not very simple because Africa is of course not very simple either.

MARTI: What I really wanted to find out is what you hope for the future of Uganda and how the people will work for Africa?

OKELLO: It's very difficult. There's hope somewhere and it's a hope that . . . some people believe they are sufficiently intelligent to be able to control life forces in other people . . . it would appear to me that there is something basically very presumptuous about people, somebody sitting down and saying, 'I'll contain nature, I'll contain life'. Basically I'm saying that there is a life force in the African which will wake up. Already it seems to me it's quite alert. Africans are in a very difficult position. They're in a situation where they're not left alone. Even the Americans were left alone for some time. Much of the idea behind isolationism was to be left alone, to have as little infiltration as possible, in order to be able to work out some kind of direction . . .' to organize ourselves, to decide, 'Where shall we go?' The Africans haven't very much of a choice sometimes. There are too many embassies around. There are too many advisers, too many scholars, too many international agencies, too many corporations, too many cynical people. And people are supposed to make up their minds in this context, have to act in this context. There are too many guns around. We don't make these guns. They come from somewhere and they threaten the lives of our people. We use them against ourselves. . . .

(*At which point the tape ends*)

Gabriel Okara

▼▼▼▼▼▼▼▼▼▼▼▼▼▼▼▼▼▼▼▼▼▼▼▼▼▼▼▼▼▼▼▼

African Speech . . . English Words

[1963]

TRYING to express ideas even in one's own language is difficult because what is said or written often is not exactly what one had in mind. Between the birth of the idea and its translation into words, something is lost. The process of expression is even more difficult in the second language of one's own cultural group. I speak not of merely expressing general ideas, but of communicating an idea to the reader in the absolute or near absolute state in which it was conceived. Here, you see I am already groping for words to make you understand what I really mean as an African.

'Once an African, always an African; it will show in whatever you write' says one school of thought. This implies that there is no need for an African writer to exert a conscious effort to make his writing African through the use of words or the construction of sentences. Equally it seems to say that the turns of phrase, the nuances and the imagery which abound in African languages, thinking, and culture are not worth letting the world know about.

As a writer who believes in the utilization of African ideas, African philosophy and African folk-lore and imagery to the fullest extent possible, I am of the opinion the only way to use them effectively is to translate them almost literally from the African language native to the writer into whatever European language he is using as his medium of expression. I have endeavoured in my words to keep as close as possible to the vernacular expressions. For, from a word, a group of words, a sentence and even a name in any African language, one can glean the social norms, attitudes and values of a people.

In order to capture the vivid images of African speech, I had to eschew the habit of expressing my thoughts first in English. It was difficult at first, but I had to learn. I had to study each Ijaw expression I used and to discover the probable situation in which it was used in order to bring out the nearest meaning in English. I found it a fascinating exercise.

Some words and expressions are still relevant to the present-day life of the world, while others are rooted in the legends and tales of a far-gone day. Take the expression 'he is timid' for example. The equivalent in Ijaw is 'he has no chest' or 'he has no shadow'. Now a person without a chest in the physical sense can only mean a human that does not exist. The idea becomes clearer in the second translation. A person who does not cast a shadow of course does not exist. All this means is that a timid person is not fit to live. Here, perhaps, we are hearing the echoes of the battles in those days when the strong and the brave lived. But is this not true of the world today?

In parting with a friend at night a true Ijaw would say, 'May we live to see ourselves tomorrow.' This again is reminiscent of the days when one went about with the danger of death from wild beasts or hostile animals dogging one's steps. But has the world we live in changed so much? On the other hand, how could an Ijaw born and bred in England, France or the United States write, 'May we live to see ourselves tomorrow' instead of 'Goodnight'? And if he wrote 'Goodnight', would he be expressing an Ijaw thought? Is it only the colour of one's skin that makes one an African?

In the Ibo language they say something like, 'May dawn come', or 'May it dawn'. Once again it is a wish or a prayer. Isn't the grave sometimes likened to an endless night and is it not only the dead that go to the grave? The Ibos sometimes lighten this sombre thought with the expression, 'You sleep like a rat while I sleep like a lizard.' Because it is thought that rats never sleep, while lizards are heavy sleepers, this never fails to produce peals of laughter.

Why should I not use the poetic and beautiful, 'May we live to see ourselves tomorrow' or, 'May it dawn', instead of 'Goodnight?' If I were writing a dialogue between two friends, one about to leave after visiting the other at night, I would do it this way:

'Are you getting up now?' said Otutu as he saw his friend heaving himself up with his two hands gripping the arms of the chair he was sitting on.

'Yes I am about walking now. The night has gone far', Beni his friend said, for he was a very fat man.

'May we live to see ourselves tomorrow', Otutu said after seeing his friend to the door.

'May we live to see ourselves tomorrow', his friend also said and walked panting into the night.

What emerges from the examples I have given is that a writer can use the idioms of his own language in a way that is understandable in English. If he uses their English equivalents, he would not be expressing African ideas and thoughts, but English ones.

Some may regard this way of writing in English as a desecration of the language. This is of course not true. Living languages grow like living things, and English is far from a dead language. There are American, West Indian, Australian, Canadian and New Zealand versions of English. All of them add life and vigour to the language while reflecting their own respective cultures. Why shouldn't there be a Nigerian or West African English which we can use to express our own ideas, thinking and philosophy in our own way?

David Rubadiri

▼▼▼▼▼▼▼▼▼▼▼▼▼▼▼▼▼▼▼▼▼▼▼▼▼▼▼▼▼▼▼

Why African Literature?

[1964]

REVIEWS and fly covers have gone to town selling in unclear but gaudy terms and colours the 'most excellent novels or poems that show the race problem at its deepest and give us an understanding of what it feels like to be involved in this tragic situation'. The terms of judgement are in themselves emotive; the words strike a new vocabulary of criticism – the race 'problem'; 'deep insight into'; 'tragic situation' – bundles of stock words like these are coming out of Africa from both white and black critics. Africa as a literary theme is now moving away from politics to become in itself a creative theme. This in itself is good. The point of this new literary trend is a healthy thing.

Writing in Africa is already showing a varied pattern of insights and views and an enormous assortment of styles. Publishers have realized this and manuscripts with African names are regarded in some printing houses as 'box office'. One can therefore only speculate when one is considering the whole question of literature and society in Africa today. It might be helpful to start with a few comments on three great novelists who I think have successfully managed to portray characters belonging to cultural groups outside of their town: E. M. Forster, William Faulkner and Joseph Conrad.

Conrad commenting on a critic's statement that writers who want a setting for their work in far off countries produce 'de-civilized' tales, said in a preface note to *Almayer's Folly* 'the critic and judge seem to think that in those distant lands all joy is a yell and a war dance, all pathos is a howl and a ghastly grin of filed teeth; and that the solution of all problems is found in the barrel of a revolver or on the point of an assegai. This is not so – and health like ours must endure the load of the gifts from heaven, the course of facts, the blessing of illusions, the bitterness of our wisdom and the deceptive consolation of our folly.' Conrad's greatness as an artist lies in his disinclination to recognize boundaries in human nature. Mrs Almeyer for instance is superstitious and depraved, but that is not because of her half-caste blood. On the other hand, William Faulkner's Joe Christmas shows an interesting Negro response to white benevolence, as for example in the following passage: 'It was not the hard work which he hated, nor the punishment and injustice, he was used to that before he ever saw either of them. He expected no less, and so was neither outraged nor surprised. It was the woman (Mrs McEachern): That soft kindness which he believed himself doomed to be forever victim of and which he hated worse than he did the hard and ruthless justice of man.' Joe Christmas goes on to kill his guardian and run away. His sex life with women (black and white) is violent. The knowledge that he has Negro blood haunts him and gives him passionate delight in seducing white women whom he recognizes as the symbol of the white man's superiority. He performs orgies with Mrs Burden and to get out of this woman's possessive love, Joe Christmas kills her, but as in all true tragedy Joe is struck down and lynched.

The point I want to make here is that this is not just a race relations story, even within the narrow boundaries of the Deep South culture with its very parochial and stock attitudes, a culture forged through phases of complex personal relationships, a complex racial history, a complex balance of racial values, and the new challenge of a people faced with problems that must be faced. These are totally new people in a totally new country with the guilt of near genocide of the red Indian – Joe Christmas is not just a Negro whose problems are externalized in terms of racial discrimination. The big problem is inside Joe Christmas himself more than within the bare situation of colour conflict.

Dr Aziz in Mr Forster's novel *A Passage to India*, Faulkner's Joe Christmas, Conrad's Nina are memorable literary creations because they cannot be hewn and carved to fit into the framework of local politics. They are characters because they were endowed with observable dimensions; they have human characteristics which have permanence and which suffer and endure historical change.

What then is the relevance of all this to major literature in Africa today? I propose to discuss a few sample works, divided into three African literary regions. Southern African; Western Africa (English speaking); and Western Africa (French speaking).

If we accept that the themes that will excite the artists in Africa for a long time to come will be:

(a) Race;
(b) The self-consciousness that comes with a search for identity; and
(c) Politics,

let us see how the white novelist tackles these conflicts. Alan Paton, perhaps the most popular South African novelist, tries to resolve all this in his novel *Cry the Beloved Country*. The novel is in many ways unique for being the first work in the history of South Africa in which a black man is the main character; and yet what do we have in this novel? A story in which the characters, that is the people who really matter, are of secondary importance. They all seem to be pathetically flat; as we read on we are saddled with the load of the author's monumental sermon on 'Comfort in desolation' . . . 'So in my suffering I can believe', is all that Rev Stephen Kumalo seems to say throughout much of the book. Mr Paton's commentator Msimangu remains untouched by the events in the story. Both characters are cloaked in a Christlike atmosphere, and they behave with a naïveté of children. They hardly develop. They are always trembling with humility and accepting the scheme of things as a matter of course. Even after his bitter experience in the city, Kumalo can still address the white boy from Jarvis' farm as 'Inkosana' (Little master). This has been the general trend of most white writers in Africa today, a pattern that begins with an evangelical missionary zeal in the white man's image of the non-white and is justified by an assumption that they know the answers not only for themselves but also for the poor natives. They need to justify not only themselves but also the black man; the Kumalo type role is highly sentimental – and one most attractive to the white novelist with a liberal tarnish. In the midst of so much pain, fear and dishonesty, he seems to say *here* is a black man who does not hate you, who harbours no bitterness. And he is a black man, too, one of the race that is often despised. Have you no reverence for such dignity? And so on. Sophiatown, the slum of flick knives, violence, debauchery, dissipation, of violent jazz and kwela, leaves Mrs Lithebe an almost angelic figure. She is untouched by it; she fits into this sermon and must not get out of hand. The tremendous forces and complications that face the boy Absalon and his mistress do not seem to really matter to the total complex of this violent situation. We are hardly allowed to see Absalon's demoralization growing. We do not even know what he thinks about himself and the social order in which he has been clamped as in a vice. When we come face to face with him, he is a frightened young man being sacrificed, waiting in jail for the hangman the next morning, as in the biblical image of the sacrifice of the young Isaac by Abraham. The image, the message, the sentiment that matters, the conflict that must bring violent power to the final totality are hardly exploited by the writer. The characters in themselves, as people, do not seem to count for much. Contrast, for instance, how Nadine Gordimer in *World of Strangers*, handles this theme in a sentence. With an urgency that jolts and satisfies she bursts out, 'I don't want to be bothered with the black man's troubles.' Or, for that matter Joyce Cary in *Mr Johnson*.

On the African side in South Africa Peter Abrahams stands high on the list. His early novels, *Dark Testament*, *Song of the City*, *Mine Boy*, are all in the Richard Wright tradition. One of his most successful novels though is *Wild Conquest*, a novel based on the story of the Great Trek. The urgency in this novel at times makes the style erratic and patchy, but he gives us introspection and characters who have lives of their own, capable of expansion. But even Abrahams does bother us in some of his passages – for example, in the following:

> 'No, my friend not mad. He is a human being now. The love that is between him and that girl has made him human. The inhibitions caused by the oppression have left him. If it were possible he would become a complex person in a very short time, but anything might happen between now and then. The tragedy is not in Swartz and his girl, the tragedy is in this land and in our time. You must be first a native or a half-caste or a Jew or an Arab or an Englishman or a Chinaman or a Greek, that is the tragedy. You cannot be a human being first . . . for that reason Swartz and this girl who have now become human beings will suffer.'

We of course accept this situation where an underdog is speaking to another underdog, but surely it is just this kind of protest which limits the emotional and intellectual range of characterization. The total framework of the novel has been chalked out for us; the situations are familiar. We know we are in a country which considers it a crime for two people with different pigmentation to fall in love with each other. The temptations to overplay the situation somehow detract from the impact of the characters. Abraham overplays in this novel the ready-made group attitudes and responses. There is an excessive play of fate in the lives of the characters and, as a result, their experience becomes a minute fraction of life. On the other hand, however, Fieta the coloured woman who emerges from a dissipated life and grows to know and accept the importance of her love for crippled Mad Sam whose own life is perpetual pain, is interesting as a character. The image of Fieta is not limited by any impending disaster from outside herself or from Mad Sam, although these impending disasters loom large and engulf the total lives of these two people. Their image is capable of development. Here again we know that they are underdogs and this makes them vulnerable. There is a wide area of self-response open to them and to the reader. Their conception has no bounds.

One can understand the tremendous desire to justify one's position in society. It is probably this that has tempted the African angry young men writing today to continually try to 'assert' and to 'declare'. In many ways this temptation has been too strong. This literature of protest, assertion and declamation has produced writing which lacks balanced sensitivity and has tended to cloud the understanding of values which, above all, society requires of an artist. It would be too risky to generalize here, but a few examples might help to prove the point. In William Conton's *The African*, a novel by an educated man in the truest sense of the term, one is shocked by the rather phoney and naïve situations that repeatedly appear. As a piece of writing it is on the whole beautiful and polished. And although one can understand Conton's rebellion against his Durham University Department of English culture, one is hard put to accept what he brings forward as the alternative: the African way of life. The author calls it 'the rediscovery of Africa'; and he sees this achieved in the total breakaway from manifestations of what he considers the Western way of life. His main character decides to go to school without shoes, discards the use of knives and forks and tables, throws out chairs, tables, mattresses, the lot, and ends up by becoming a polygamist without telling us why. He barely takes us into his confidence to tell us the spiritual conflicts that must have been undergone throughout this personal development of the self, of the man who now wants to be a real African. I find it very difficult to accept this. The artist after all must be the sensitive point of his community or society and though he must begin from self, he is at the same time expressing the genuine longings, failings, conflicts, and successes of its being. It is this trend to assert, this concept of negritude ; a word that has become currency in African literary criticism and one which in many cases is used loosely to embrace all Negro art and the Negroness or blackness of African artistic activities, that must be stopped before it gains power as a value judgement. I feel the concept has served its purpose; but the danger is still there. This is especially true of French speaking Africa, where the assimilated African has been forced to think of himself in the first instance as being a Frenchman. In this concept of negritude he believes he sees the only way of asserting a dignity which never can be asserted by other 'slogans'.

I think that negritude is dangerous because its final result is to press down the creative spirit, to tie it, sometimes so tight that a work of art becomes meaningless. President Léopold Sédar Senghor, an advocate of negritude, a good poet in many ways, sometimes even goes to the extent of saying: 'Emotion is at the heart of negritude, emotion is Negro.' With all good grace this is only absurdly untrue. One can form a literary cult in Africa but such cults should not be asserted by emotion, like, for instance, in a poem which Senghor wrote on a visit to New York. In this poem Senghor is contrasting Manhattan with Harlem, the Negro quarter of New York.

Manhattan
No mother's breast, but only nylon legs. Legs and breasts
  That have no sweat or smell

No tender word have they no lips only artificial hearts
    Paid for in hard cash.
Nights of insomnia or nights of Manhattan! So agitated by
    Flickering lights, where motor horns howl of empty hours,
And while dark waters carry away hygienic loves
    Like rivers flooded with corpses of children.

Harlem

Harlem! Harlem! Harlem! Now I say Harlem! A green
    Breeze of corn springing up from pavements ploughed by
The naked feet of dancers.
    Bottoms, waves of silk and sword blade breasts, water-lily,
Ballets and fabulous masks.

Well! We are asked to believe that Manhattan women are just 'scented crocodiles'. And Harlem, which we know is a den of misery, debauchery, poverty and oppression; stinking of overcrowded flats, filled with sprawling hungry children, we are asked to accept as 'a green breeze of corn'. Even when one knows that the spirit of Jazz throbs in Harlem, this is negritude gone mad. One can hardly, even with Madame Senghor, his French wife behind our minds, accept the genuineness of this contrast. 'Sweat' and 'smell' may have their romantic charms, but the desire here to explain away a nagging negative statement which dark sensibility has often resented, that black men stink, is surely propaganda. A French Guinean poet writes in one of his poems called *Black Doll*:

        Give me my black dolls
        To disperse
        The image of pale wenches, vendors of love
        Going and coming
        On the boulevards of my boredom.

In another poem by Leon Damas, called *The Balance Sheet* he says:

        I feel ridiculous
        In their shoes in their dinner jackets
        In their stiff shirts and paper collars,
        With monocles and bowler hats
        I feel ridiculous with my toes that were not made
        To sweat from morning to evening
        In their swaddling clothes that weaken my limbs
        and deprive my body of its beauty.

When you come to think of it, any self-respecting nudist of any race could declare this. It would not make them any less of whatever nationality they happened to be.

Much of this sentiment about negritude is sheer romanticism; often it is mawkish and strikes a pose. When a poet like Aimé Césaire describes the following in one of his poems one begins to wonder!

> Hail the Royal Kailcedrat! Hail those who have invented nothing,
> Who have explored nothing, but they abandon themselves
>   possessed by the very essence of all things,
> Heedless of tanning, but playing the game of the world.

It is difficult to be asked to take the sentiments of this poem seriously. Are we to believe that our best lot is to lie down in the jungles, basking in the sun, waiting for bananas to fall in our mouths? Is this really us? And is this really negritude?

In 1941 a Zulu poet wrote a romantic poem of about a thousand lines in English. He called it *The Valley of a Thousand Hills*. The valley of a thousand hills is there, it is in Natal province, perhaps one of the most beautiful scenes in South Africa. The poem is Dhlomo's struggle to understand himself, an underdog, the meaning of pain, despair, confusion, power and greed. In it he sees the plight of the South African non-white, the suffering of man. His protest imagery is drawn from Byron and Shelley, and his nostalgic melancholy from Keats. He too has a bird in this valley that sings a song that never was heard before by man.

> From whence you come, pain, beauty, love and joy
> Have mingled out into a bloom of song!
> But here on earth man's soul remains the toy
> Of unharmonious processes which long
> Have raged; here where our youth and joys are mocked
> By want and tears, where like the dead, foul dust
> Shut tight the door, where age, deemed wise, is rocked
> By scourge of fear and hate!

Then he discovers the importance of self:

> Our world, our thoughts, our all is in the self
> God is as great as the individual soul!
> Our bigness makes life bog; our smallness, cringed
> Not God or man or Devil or the world,
> But self chastises or enthrones the soul.
> Our God or Devil is the feeling self,
> Catastrophe or life the self-same self,
> Thus I am God! And God is I . . . this self!
> So purity and peace reigned everywhere

Deep in the Valley of a Thousand Hills
For purity and peace in me then reigned.

Here is a small glimpse, perhaps of romanticism and the spontaneous inclination to dramatics which pervades the African character. The fatalism which embraces the African, to face and carry the tragic moment, making a character at once submissive and violent, accommodating and uncompromising, full of laughter and tears, it is impossible to define. One can only search for the African personality, and society demands this from its artists, much more from its writers. The literature of 'assertion' and 'protest' could easily be a negative factor in a society that teems with so much life and creative spirit.

Our literary young men can now begin to write prose and verse that flows from the wells of the creative spirit, untied by the desire to justify African conflicts by mere surface solutions. Colour is important. But a painter is needed to create a true masterpiece.

Sembène Ousmane, Cheikh Hamidou Kane, Ousmane Socé, Tchicaya U Tam'si, Camara Laye, Birago Diop, and Abdou Anta Ka

▼▼▼▼▼▼▼▼▼▼▼▼▼▼▼▼▼▼▼▼▼▼▼▼▼

The Writers Speak

[1965]

GOLLIET: M. Sembène Ousmane has kindly agreed to say a few words about his own work and the questions we have been discussing.

OUSMANE: I will begin with the questions we have been discussing. A whole number of problems have been raised on which, it seems to me, we have heard the views of Europeans. That, I think, has been a bad mistake, unless all the Africans have run away. I should have preferred it if the reports and texts had been presented by Africans. It would have given us a more comprehensive view of the works dealt with. Referring to a book need not imply any criticism of it and I should like to say a word about the *Adventure Ambiguë*. I am not proposing to discuss the actual text because, in order to comment at all on the spiritual experiences of the hero, or his anguish, wanderings and solitude, one must first know the origins of the Fulahs, their innate feudal tradition and their deep religious sense. What I do think is, however, that if the exposé had been made by an African it would have had a more positive meaning both for the Africans and for the Europeans. Then one speaker said that literature should keep clear of politics. I do not agree. I am not here to represent Senegal; I am not representing anyone but myself, Sembène Ousmane, although I belong to Senegal. We are speaking French and the word 'politique' means the affairs of the City and, it is impossible to discuss the art and culture of living men in isolation from the men themselves. To try to analyse Cheikh Hamidou Kane's book apart from its social, economic or religious setting seems to me to make no sense.

So much for that. Now let me go on to another question, that of negritude. Apparently, I have been going in for negritude without realizing it, which is quite a surprise. What is negritude? Speaking for myself, here in Senegal, the very centre of negritude, I say frankly that I do not know. Why don't I know? If we look at the social situation in Senegal today – mind, I say the social situation – nothing seems to have been achieved at all. So far as I am concerned, negritude reminds me of that 'folfol' worn by women expecting a baby which lets you see their whole body through their clothes. Negritude seems to me to have nothing solid about it. What it may become in future is another question. There was a time when negritude meant something positive. It was our breastplate against a culture that wanted at all costs to dominate us. But that is past history. In 1959 some of us who called ourselves writers, on the strength of having managed to get a book or a couple of short stories into print, were already opposing negritude. I would like to refer you to a book by the Belgian writer, Madame Kesteloot, in which you will find many references to it. For my part, I do not believe negritude has a future. Every form of culture, especially literature, has its own ideology, so the problem is a political one. The one exception, if I may say so without flattery, is a single book, or collection of short stories, by Amadou Koumba, which shows no trace of anything traditional. Other books refer to the emotion or the sensibility, or other phenomena, said to characterize the black races. I do not believe in this. There are things that do truly characterize the black races, I agree, but no one has yet worked out exactly what they are and no really thorough study of negritude has ever been undertaken, because negritude neither feeds the hungry nor builds roads. Another thing I strongly disapprove of is the report by one of the participants in this colloquy in which the author says that he has conducted an inquiry in Casamance to discover what negritude means. I call that dishonest and also a great display of ignorance on his part, because the people he was questioning could neither read nor write. As he is a university man himself, he would have got better information by asking university people to tell him what negritude was. I am against negritude because to me nowadays it no longer means that combination of revolutionary fervour that people like to pretend that it has. I will not say more because I am preparing something myself on negritude, so I will await your questions.

As for my own books – I must not go on talking indefinitely – everyone here has turned to writing for different reasons. Some say they need to express themselves, some that they have an urge to write; but, so far as I am concerned, writing, which is now my job, is a social necessity, like the jobs of the mason, the carpenter, or the iron-worker.

With regard to the other point raised I think that until we have made the African languages part of our educational system, in the primary schools and elsewhere, our literature will still be subject to the control of other powers, or other people's good intentions. Even here, since mention has been made of Dakar University, what we have is only a continuation of the French university. This does not seem to me to be a good thing and, if you ask me why, I would say that it is because the people who come here, despite all they can do, have no regular contact with the mass of the people, not even with their own students. I know this is true because during the two or three days I have been in Dakar I have been making inquiries from the professors about how much contact they have with their students, and the answer is that, outside the classes, there is no contact at all. Apart from the classes, they never see their students and this is merely another example of what we are always denouncing as cultural imperialism.

GOLLIET: Thank you. I hope you will be kind enough to answer one or two questions.

DIOP: I have no questions, but my native language is Wolof and I would like to ask M. Sembène Ousmane to repeat the whole of his speech in Wolof. That is all. He talks about cultural imperialism. Very well, I would just like him to make the same speech, as eloquently, in Wolof.

OUSMANE: Here we have the proof that all of us who are writers are also people who have to some extent lost their roots because I can repeat a part of what I said but, for the rest, I should have to bring in foreign words. But I do not think that means that our language is poorer. There are some things that we did not discover when we came into the world because certain forces held us back. But there are things we can add to our languages. Since we claim to benefit from all revolutions, I am not in favour of shutting ourselves up completely in a black world, in negritude. If we want an open window on to all races and all languages, we must also borrow from others. Every language has borrowed from every other; French is a rich language but even it has its foreign words. You go to Paris, so you must listen to the 'radio', you must visit 'les self-services', 'les nightclubs', and all the rest. Don't you? (Applause.) What can't be cured must be endured . . . or improved.

DIOP: Yes, but you are suffering from exactly the complex we have to get rid of – colonialism, imperialism, neo-colonialism. . . . All that. I ask you to address me in Wolof, to make your speech over again in Wolof and you come back at me with a kind of cultural demagogy.

OUSMANE: I can assure you that, if I had taken the time, I could have written *Le Docker Noir* in Wolof. But then who would have read it? How many people know how to read the language? And if I had not taken the trouble at least to learn the grammar, even if only phonetically, I should not be in a position to write it; but then who is going to read me? And how many people, I speak only of Africans, is it going to affect? That is one of the contradictions of our life. Very well, then. Even written in French, how many Africans have read *Le Docker Noir*? You were hearing this morning from the Chairman of my first conversation in Paris about the sale of African literature. And let me point out, it is not a case of saying that all black people are literate. Eighty-five per cent of the people here are illiterate; the rest can read and write but they do not read African authors. That means that our public is in Europe. My sensibilities are different from those of a European. That is inevitable. It is not merely the colour of our respective skins, because there are differences between other peoples as well. The sensibilities of a Dane will differ from those of a Lapp. So will those of a Negro from Senegal from those of one from New Guinea, a Papou. But if you are going to talk about negritude, you must ask the Papou what he thinks about it as well. What distinguishes *Le Docker Noir* is that, when I was writing it, I was already in exile from my home and working – as had been the case for some time – and I needed to attract someone's attention. At that time, the present President of Senegal was the leader of the Independent Group in the National Assembly. I went to see him because I was then the secretary of the *Travailleurs de France* for Marseilles and I wanted to raise this problem with him. But if you read *Le Docker Noir* carefully, you will see that the problem was not merely the position of the Negroes it was that of the Arabs and the Spanish exiles as well. All right, no comparison is possible between my sensibilities and those of the Whites: true enough, but do not say, because of that, that I support negritude.

ANTA KA: I have a question to put to M. Sembène. It seems to me, M. Sembène, that the time for these big words is past. This cultural imperialism we hear about – men being what they are and history being what it is, it is unavoidable. And a good thing too, for the whole of the rest of the world. So this is the problem, M. Sembène. You have written *Le Docker Noir*, you have written *Les bouts de bois de Dieu*, as well as a number of other things, including your last book, *Les Voltaïque*. The African has already gone a long way towards freedom; do you not think he may get tired of being reminded that he is an ex-colonial, that he has been subject to political and cultural influences, etc? Do you not think that literature is something different from politics, particularly from the type of politics that consists in always drawing attention to grievances? From the people I meet – the Dogons, the Voltaiques, the Mossi, the Casamanci and the Wolofs and the Toucouleurs – it seems to me that they are much happier talking about themselves and without even thinking of this cultural sentimentalism you talk about. Besides, I should not like this debate to take a political turn. It must be kept at a literary level and everyone must say exactly what he thinks. That is more important than anything.

OUSMANE: Abdou Anta Ka says I tire my readers. All right, but as unfortunately it seems that I have no readers in Africa I think it is a little out of place for him to speak. If it were a European raising the point of whether or not I tired my readers by introducing so much politics, that would be another matter. But, as I see it, the whole thing is interconnected. After all, what is pure literature?

GOLLIET: I should like to ask Cheikh Hamidou Kane what he thinks.

KANE: You want to know what I think about negritude. Well, I think it is a moment in the cultural evolution of the black world. I say a moment, but I mean a decisive moment; I do not mean that negritude is a kind of grill through which all present and future work by black artists must automatically be examined. It seems to me that this theme, or rather this flag of negritude was something that we had no choice but to raise at a certain given moment in our evolution. I do not reject it; I do not deny its utility. We had, at some point, to make ourselves felt, if we were ever to make ourselves known and refuse cultural or political assimilation, especially at a time when, politically speaking, we had no prospects of an early liberation. That, I think, explains why the concept or theme of negritude ever emerged. I can quite understand why, since then, either out of habit or because it seemed convenient, we should have gone on attaching everything that happened to the same theme but, if we are to go on doing it, we must be clear exactly what it is we are doing. I believe there to be a Negro aesthetic, and perhaps black artists also have their own characteristic sensibility or way of approach; but to say that these permanent factors represent the whole dimension or characteristics of *negritude* seems to me to be confusing the container with its contents. Once again, I do not reject negritude in any way. None of us – no African writer, poet, man of letters or novelist – can, I think, deny the deep impression made on him by Aimé Césaire, Léopold Senghor, Paul Niger and many others; and the reason for the depth of that impression is that they have been the standard bearers of negritude. They sounded the first trumpet-call, as it were. But, it seems to me, the time is coming when, without wishing to deny any of that, we must nevertheless give up trying to bring everything down to it, unless we wish to become completely hidebound. To act otherwise would itself, I think, be a new form of imperialism. Moreover, it would also be to split the solidarity that unites us with the rest of mankind. I will come back to that in a moment. We African writers, writing in a non-African language, are like a series – if I may be allowed the expression – of geological strata one on top of the other, simply because we are Africans. It has happened that a number of religions, originating outside Africa, have been superimposed on our own traditional religious beliefs, which they have not, incidentally, always succeeded in eradicating. And, furthermore, we have had imposed on us a non-African culture. So each of us is the sum of all those. In such circumstances, to see only the Negro in us may, I think, be to some extent to mutilate us. On the other hand, it is equally important not to try to root out all the Negro in us either. But that is not really the problem. I myself, in addition to the characteristic I have in common with all my racial brothers, also have other characteristics that link me to those of my racial brothers who share them with me. There are not so many of those. I am a Moslem; not every black man is a Moslem. I am a Toucouleur; not every black man is a Toucouleur. I have been schooled in the West; not every black man has been schooled in the West – by that I mean in the school of Western Europe. And there, I think, lies my problem. I cannot reject, I cannot deliberately get rid of these elements in myself. I am obliged to accept them, and that not just in theory but as part of my daily life. I think this is to some extent reflected in my book, and not only there but in all my actions. There is nothing deliberate about this; it is just my life.

There has been some discussion here about the use of the African languages. What I have just said, I think, bears on that problem. It may well be that we should have expressed our deepest feelings and problems more adequately if we had been able to do so in our own languages. You know the usual objections as well as I do. We may all have the same coloured skin which we share with no one else, but our languages are legion and are not always a means of bringing us together. Besides, our languages need modernizing and we need to learn to write them, we need to teach them and to use them. But meanwhile, until this has all been done, are we to do nothing else? Are we not to live or express ourselves? Are we to call a halt to all evolution? My own answer would be no; nor do I think there is anyone whose answer would be yes. But without exactly saying yes to these questions, it is possible to adopt a kind of half-way attitude, especially with regard to the question of sitting with our arms folded and waiting until we have forged a language of our own. It reminds me of a trap into which we were sometimes apt to fall, in the days before we had gained our independence. We used to be told that political independence implied the creation of a nation, in other words, a historical and sociological entity, and we were further told that so long as all the necessary conditions had not been fulfilled it was probably impossible that we should become independent. One of these conditions was the possession of a language. And we allowed ourselves to fall into the trap. Was it true that it was necessary to wait till we had forged 'black' languages to speak and write in before demanding independence? We have acquired our independence and now we have time to build up our languages. That is something we have to tackle. I do not say it is not something that must be done. We shall not be able fully to express our whole thought until we have done it. But until then we should be thankful that the languages we have got, that we received from our colonizers, can serve us as a means of expression and of building up the economies of our countries, a task of which no one will dispute the urgency.

SOCÉ: I will not keep you long. I only wish to say that I entirely agree with M. Cheikh Hamidou Kane's concept of negritude. His piercing analysis has successfully shown us the distinction between false negritude which is static, unbending, and the broader concept of a negritude that will be infinitely more dynamic. When considering this question of negritude, I think we should remember what Rabindranath Tagore said about culture. He said that to him culture did not mean turning one's back on other cultures, countries or civilisations; culture, to him, meant throwing one's door wide open to the spirit of every other culture but without letting oneself be carried away by it.

U TAM'SI: There have been criticisms, or attempts at criticism, of the work of some of the poets present here, including myself. I have been asked whether I agree with Gerald Moore, whether I agree with Armand Guibert, whether I agree with what Herr Jahn has said about style. What I say is that Mr Moore, M. Guibert and Herr Jahn are the doctors and I am the patient. They have made their diagnosis and what am I supposed to say next? Is it likely I shall give them the sack when I need to be cured – always supposing I do? All right, then, I shall keep them on and ask them to go on examining me and then I shall see whether they really put their finger on the problem. I am not in a position to do so myself but I shall not run away because I have, after all, some courage. I shall reply.

Another question put to me – I am speaking directly to the students present – was my attitude to negritude in relation to what I say in my poems. That implies the diagnosis that negritude can be discerned in my poetry. I have said before that my negritude was unconscious, or at least involuntary, and Herr Jahn also used the word unconscious in connection with the characteristic features of negritude, or anyhow the criteria by which he distinguished the African style in African poetry, especially my own. So be it. The way to analyse African writing nowadays is perhaps to follow a method of literary criticism very common in the nineteenth century, which involves defining a man's position first by reference to his works and only afterwards by reference to other criteria. This may suggest something to my questioners. And now let us have done with this question of negritude once for all.

Do I agree with the other points made by Mr Gerald Moore about poetry, and Herr Jahn? As I say, I do not know. The only way I can answer is to tell you how I work. I have a table, like everyone else, and I also have a typewriter, as well as a pen and ink. Lamine Diakhaté is here and he has been to see me and can tell you how he found me working. So can Guibert. There are no files with recipes in them. Accordingly, I don't consult them, I write as the mood takes me and, if you want the truth, I have no idea of how to oblige the passing mood to fall in with all that I should like to be. As to why I write – well, most writers certainly do not do so in order to get anything out of their system, or to talk about themselves. Perhaps it may be to discover something in themselves. As to what that may be, Gerald Moore has said that what he finds in my poetry is the Congo, and you have just had 'Il reste un fleuve' read to you. It is true that it is the river that interests me more than anything else because I was born not far from its banks and I wish its course and mine could be the same. That is no mean ambition, because the Congo's course is 4,500 kilometres long. I should like to come from the same source, far off, up by Louaba, on the borders of Katanga. The Congo flows into the sea, as do most rivers, and I should like to flow into the sea with it. I picture civilisations as being like rivers, all flowing into the sea to become a universal civilisation. But meanwhile, I should like to follow along 4,500 kilometres. The Seine is easily 600 kilometres long, or maybe only 200 or 300, I don't know and I don't mind, but that is the direction in which I think I want to go. Of course, there may be other things to find; one can find anything one wants to find. And if that is true, then I will find that I am a great poet, greater than I think; but if you find that the Congo is as Gerald Moore has described it, then I find that that is already a great deal. But, as far as I myself am concerned, if you find surrealism in my work, you may be right; and if you find negritude, that may be true as well.

There is one other point. For some time now, especially since my last book came out, I have been ranged alongside Césaire. I am a Congo Césaire, a Congo 'baci'. Before I came to the African writers, before I read either Césaire or Senghor, I read what I was given at school. Finally, I came across a writer who struck me as quite extraordinary, and that was Arthur Rimbaud. We have almost all read him. Rimbaud was my first master and he is still my master. Often, I have to turn back to him first, before I can turn to any of the others. If I am told that my work resembles that of Césaire, or that I have borrowed from Césaire, which may be true, I remind myself that we are living in a world in which everyone can be affected by everything, without even being near it. There is no need to live beside an atomic pile to be affected by certain rays; one can be as far as 500 kilometres away. But first there must be the atom bomb and then the atom town near by. It seems to me quite possible that Césaire has left his mark on me and that Senghor may have done the same. I have no wish to deny it. If my work is like that of Césaire, Mallarmé, Senghor and the rest, so much the better. It simply proves that I am very human, that I have not got a closed mind. That is all. And now, broadly speaking, I have told you in somewhat haphazard fashion, and not at all in theoretical terms, what I am trying to be and to do.

The Soul of Africa in Guinea

LAYE: I feel I must begin by thanking the organizers of this historic colloquy arranged by the Faculty of Letters of Dakar University. It has given us an opportunity of seeing our colleagues again, and now that I find myself once again on Senegalese soil, I reflect with pleasure that it was here in Dakar that most of the generation which is now guiding with such skill the destinies of a large part of the African continent received its education.

This most valuable meeting will certainly enable the members of the teaching profession in Africa to make the best possible use of the books that have appeared on Africa, besides perhaps giving writers on the subject a clearer insight into the part they themselves can play.

Although we are only here as observers, we thought it our duty to contribute a short paper which we have entitled *The soul of Africa in Guinea*; the soul, that is, of all of us whose home is Guinea. But I quickly found that the best way to treat the subject would be to talk about myself – to go back, I mean, to my own childhood memories and tell you how and why I came to make a book of them. I hope you will forgive me if I break with convention by continuing to talk in the first person.

When I was living in Paris, far away from Guinea where I was born, far away from my parents, leading for the most part a very solitary life that had already lasted for several years, my thoughts would often go back to my own country and my family. Then, one day, it occurred to me that although my recollections were then still fresh in my mind, they would be bound to fade in time, even if they could never – how could they? be effaced altogether. So I started writing them down. I was living alone, in a poorly-furnished student's room, and I wrote as if in a dream. I remembered and I wrote for pleasure, and it was a very great pleasure indeed and one of which I never tired.

I can still remember those evenings, long winter evenings mostly, evenings which could have been unbearably gloomy but which I found all too short. And yet they followed days which were also long and, during much of the time, devoted to unending work so that often, when I got home to my little hotel at the Porte d'Orléans, at the other end of Paris, I was feeling worn out. I am talking about a time when I had to interrupt my studies because there was no more money and I was desperately trying to earn enough to start them again. I had a job as a workman at Simca's and after finishing there I used to go on to evening classes at the Conservatoire des Arts et Métiers. The days never seemed to end, and it was cold, and I seemed to have no physical or mental energy left.

But then seated at my little table lit by one miserable lamp – why is it that hotel bedrooms always have lamps that seem to grudge one even the minimum of light? – I would sit down to write and, in my thoughts, I was back again with my friends and family, beside our great river, the Niger. That was all I needed. I felt inexpressibly happy and I no longer felt alone. I felt as though I was with my father and mother, as though we were talking to each other. I felt their warmth all round me once more. And the light over my head, shining on my table and on to the sheets of paper I was covering with my hurried scrawl, was no longer a wretched little electric bulb but the sun in Guinea, that implacable African sun whose rays I could feel.

My pen could not go fast enough. Memories jostled each other; they came so fast that my pen sometimes stopped abruptly because I did not know which recollection to take first. I wanted to take them all at once.

And sometimes it stopped because my father or my mother were actually there in front of me and I saw them again as on the day I said goodbye to them, when I literally tore myself away from them to take the plane for Paris, and because I could see the tears in their eyes. I had to stop writing; my own eyes would be full of tears and I would have a lump in my throat, but I was not unhappy. How could I be unhappy? I was with my own family, sitting in my own home, walking the roads of my native country.

And then I would begin to write again and feel again that indescribable pleasure of writing as I dreamt. When at last I went to bed, midnight would have struck hours before and I would fall asleep, my spirit a thousand miles away from Paris.

I have said that, at that time, I was only thinking of myself and my own enjoyment; that I was writing merely for pleasure and in order to feel less alone. It is true that I had then no idea of publishing a line of what I wrote. How should I have had? My ambition was a very different one – to finish my studies. My intention was to become a trained technician and go home to Africa for good. I had no idea at the time that my scribbled pages would ever be taken out of the drawer where I kept them, except for me to read over to myself in order to call up again in all their freshness, before my tired eyes, the recollections that time had faded.

Besides, all I had written, all I had dreamed, did not by any means make a book. What I had produced was a huge mass of paper covered with notes scribbled down without either order or method; recollections I had jotted down as they occurred to me in the arbitrary way that such things do. It would have required the most indulgent critic to see in this confusion the product of any kind of art. In any case, does one write one's memoirs before one reaches the end of one's life, before one is really old?

All the same, that is what finally I did, but it was almost by accident. As usual, it was all the result of a conversation. I had been enjoying large tribes – into those compact groups which made our country villages so friendly, so peaceable and so united. I am talking of the love that even extended to the background against which our lives were lived, the immense Guinea plain, the savannah, that most beautiful of all savannahs, our great river, everything that lived on that level plain and in that mighty river, everything that flew in the sky; love for the trees and crops, but also for the spirits that watched over them; love for the animals but also for our totems; love for living men but also for our ancestors; love for the heavens but also for God.

It was through that love that we remained within the mystery, and even when love seemed to be directing our life away from the mystery, that was and could only be an appearance, for there is no mystery in the absence of beings and things, any more than the mystery can be clearly or intimately apprehended without at least a beginning of love for beings and things, without some kind of almost mystical union with them.

Yesterday, in Africa, we were nearer to beings and things, and that for reasons which are not at all mysterious. Perhaps it was only because our life was less busy and we ourselves less distracted. We were shielded by having fewer artificial elements in our lives, fewer facilities. Our towns cut us off less from the country. We lived like the men of the Middle Ages, knowing nothing or almost nothing of this mechanical age, the age Europe and America are passing through.

Do not, however, on any account confuse – as is only too often done – this mechanical age with civilization itself. Civilization is something quite different. It is not to be confused with machinery and still less with bombs and inter-planetary missiles. Civilization, European, American, Asian, and our own, existed long before mechanical progress, though that does not mean that Africa refuses progress. On the contrary, she longs for it; but she regards it as merely an accessory to real civilization.

Man's body has its needs, but so has his soul and the soul, after all, comes before the body, however little the two can be separated and however little the body is to be despised.

In large towns, the accumulation of mechanical aids can easily smother the soul which is, as it were, borne down by all kinds of progress which are not its concern but the effects of which it can rarely escape. But the soul knows what is happening, it feels its chains and seeks by every means to shake them off. Some of the ways it tries are as odd I feel sure, as any to be found in our old beliefs that yesterday so surprised the European rationalists.

We must, however, be careful not to mistake the nature of their rationalism, which exists far more in their speech than in their thought. When we look at what is best and most genuine in Europe, it is not machinery that we see but books, paintings, architecture; what our ears hear is not the humming of machinery but the sound of the orchestras. What is truly deep and genuine in Europe is the message of her writers and artists, her scientists, moralists, musicians and revolutionaries. That is Europe's soul and the message is not one of rationalism. It is a message coming from the soul and nowhere else. That is true, despite the signs of rationalism to be discerned in the so-called abstract works of certain artists and musicians in Europe today; signs, moreover, which it would be hard to discern in any of her writers, because while the abstract can creep into painting and music, in literature it is revealed for what it is – complete emptiness.

You will be wondering what all this digression has been leading up to. It has simply been leading us back again to the mystery which is indissolubly linked to the soul, the invisible which without the soul could not exist in us. It has brought us back to that union between heaven and earth which we share with all civilizations and from which they all take their rise.

When writing my childhood memories I wanted them to lead me on to the ineffable, to the minute and patient search for the ineffable which is the concern of us all – the search which directs us beyond the surroundings of this mechanical age, which ties us all to the same destiny, the destiny of all human beings, none of whom are more than travellers in this world. Although my ambition far out-ran my powers, that was what I was trying to do when I decided that my book should relate all the mystery inherent in my childhood memories.

In the past, in the great over-grown village of Kouroussa in Upper Guinea, there is no doubt that the air, water, earth and savannahs were, really and truly, inhabited by genii, who had to be propitiated by prayers and sacrifices. There really were people who could bewitch you, and there were formulas for averting the ill effects of their charms. There were innumerable amulets that could be worn for protection. There were tellers of hidden things; there were healers some of whom really effected cures. All these things really did exist, surprised as our children and grandchildren will be to learn it. All these things were current yesterday in Africa and they greatly astonished the Europeans although they then possessed their own mysteries which, though they were different, should nevertheless have taught them to accept the existence of ours.

Everything I wrote down, everything I remembered, was a really true picture.

And why should it not be true?

Is there nothing to the world except what we can see at a casual glance?

Does not the true reality of the world consist precisely in what cannot be seen at a glance?

Is life everything?

Is death nothing?

Has life nothing behind it?

Does death finish everything?

Is death at the end of everything?

Think what a life would be that was to be finished by death! Think what a vast swindle our life and all its activity would be! Is such a swindle conceivable?

I refuse to believe it. Our soul refuses to believe it. And so, it is in all the rest that I prefer to believe, however surprising it may seem to us when we happen to think of it in our worser moments, when we are no longer ourselves, when our soul ceases to vibrate, and our whole being becomes sluggish, or is animated by some unreasoning or over-reasoning logic.

My whole being cries out for wonders, for prodigies, and when I recognize their presence I know that it is the better part of myself awakening, my whole self.

The visible world shrinks suddenly before my eyes; I watch it dwindling into what it is, a dream and yet not quite a dream. But the sign, the sign of what exists beyond, of what is higher, infinitely higher, than the sign which itself is only appearance, is nothing, nothing that can satisfy. . . . I see the invisible rise up and confound our poor little reason which can only claim so tiny a place; I see the inexplicable elevated once more to its seat which is supreme above all.

At last I see the soul! . . . I recognize the soul!

And I know that there are more things, many more things, in heaven than those we are aware of on earth.

But I see I cannot speak of mystery without speaking also of sculpture, African sculpture, examples of which are to be found today in all the principal museums of the world and which served yesterday, even more fully than African literature, to reveal the extraordinary deep sympathies hidden in the heart of the African.

Let me begin by reminding you that, confronted with African sculpture which had not yet won a place in the history of art but whose influence had suddenly spread like a tidal wave, yesterday's artists, who have now become the great artists of today, had no other thought than of the new plastic forms to which it had introduced them. These they seized on avidly for their experiments. because they offered the possibility of all kinds of new tricks and new combinations. But what the discovery of African sculpture did not lead them to was any increase in spirituality. That is why, looking back to thirty or forty years ago and the experiments artists were carrying out at that time, the effects of which have in large measure persisted to the present day, we find nothing but a new form, a new style, neither better nor worse than its predecessors.

When I was going to primary school in Kouroussa, about 1940 or 1941, after school was over I used to enjoy going into my father's workshop and finding him, adze in hand, chipping away at the wood. There was something I always used to find curious and that I did not understand until years later. My father did not copy the model in front of him;

he transposed it. Sometimes this process of transposition went so far that something abstract crept into his work. By that, I do not mean abstract to the point of disguising the subject but I mean something not introduced intentionally and that consequently bore no relation to what is now known in Europe as abstract painting or abstract sculpture. It only appeared occasionally in my father's work and seemed more like expressionism pressed to its furthest limits, even uncertain perhaps what those limits were.

Crouched over his carving, my father transposed from his model without any calculation. He left his heart to speak as it felt, with the result that he would alter the appearance of the original, thus first drawing attention to, and accentuating the expression, the spirituality, which in its turn led to other alterations, in the actual shape this time, designed to balance and complete the original one.

I think it may be worthwhile to pause for a moment over these alterations. As I have said, they were not made without cause, they were needed to achieve a certain given spiritual expression. You will ask, if they were not made without cause and were not just a trick, how is it that they are ordered in such masterly fashion in all our carvings from Africa? Why are the planes and volumes in African sculpture so much better balanced than in any other? Why do they remind us of variations on a given theme? Why is the rhythm – at last we have reached the word – why is the rhythm so infinitely more arresting than in any other type of sculpture?

Here, we have reached one of the most important aspects of the African soul. As the president of Senegal himself reminded us here yesterday, it is rhythm – the love of it and the gift of it – that enables us to play the tom-toms instinctively, without ever having been taught, that prevents us from ever hearing those drums without wanting to dance, which makes us all born musicians and born dancers. But I am not going to do more than touch on that subject; for there is too much that I could say on it.

Again, perhaps, you will ask what was the use of the little figure that would shape itself under my father's adze . . . what good was it at that time? Well, yesterday – I am talking of the years 1940 to 1941 – the head, the little figure, the animal carved by my father, everything that our various metal workers made, was inseparable from the mystery; it was directly connected with the cult, with magic. It was a time when the smith-sculptor was also a priest and the art he practised was far more than that of a simple craftsman because it involved working with fire throughout, to smelt the ore and to work the metal. The weapons he produced were able to wound not only because they were sharp and well-tempered, but because the power to cut and wound had been given them. The hoe of the peasant was not simply the tool with which he turned the earth; it was the tool that ordered the earth and the harvest. It was a time when the art of the smith far outstripped the other arts, was more noble than they, was indeed a noble art, the art of the first of the magicians, an art which in truth called for greater knowledge and skill than the rest.

In our society it is likely that the smith was, in fact, the first specialized craftsman. The knowledge called for, the number of operations through which the ore must pass before it can be transformed into a weapon or farm implement, all mean specialization. And once a smith's skill was recognized, naturally it was to him one went when one wanted something carved – not a simple bowl that anyone can make for himself, but statues of one's ancestors, including the farthest back of all, the totem, or masks for ritual dances; all the cultural objects, in short, that his powers allowed him to consecrate.

If the smith has never ceased to possess those powers, it must nevertheless be admitted that they have become generally much weakened and that this has been inevitable in a society whose own civilization has been confronted with a whole series of new ideas. Nor is it that the notion of mystery has disappeared; it is that the mystery itself is no longer to be found in the same place. It has emigrated.

I realized this myself one day in 1956, after I had come back to Africa for good, when I went to see my father in Upper Guinea. I remember my astonishment at finding him that day once again whittling away at a piece of wood, and how I tried to guess what the block of wood was destined to become as I listened to the quick, regular strokes of his tool. But I had need of all my patience before I knew whether I had guessed right. The wood was so hard it was like marble and the work took a long time to complete. And yet there was little mystery about it. It was merely the head of an African woman which at last emerged almost unexpectedly from the wood. Suddenly, in the mass I perceived an outline and understood what it was that was growing out of it. The mystery, in fact, ended there. It was not a very mysterious mystery. It was the reply to a riddle I had set myself.

And what about my father? What was he seeking as he shaped and hollowed the wood? Reality. He was seeking to be true; as true as it is possible to be. His search for truth and reality was tempered only by his search for ideal beauty and, as a corollary, for the creation of a type of universal beauty. So that, of this woman's face, he had made the most beautiful woman's face and consequently an idealized face which summed up all faces; a universal type.

You will see at once that this is a search for reality of a somewhat special kind as it does not admit the representation of ugliness which would fight against the idealism.

But what a difference between the form that emerged in 1940 or 1941 and the form that emerged in 1956! By the time Guinea had been declared independent in 1958, what a distance had been traversed and what a gulf separated the present from the past! What trouble preceded the opening of the new era!

Through colonization, French civilization has taught us a language that we shall carefully preserve. But there is also much it has taken away from our own civilization.

Under the guidance of our President, His Excellency Sekou Touré, the first thing we did, after independence, was to take hold of ourselves again. Very quickly, we picked up again our own music, our own literature, our own sculpture; all, that is to say, that was most deeply implanted in us and that had been slumbering during the sixty years of our colonization. That is our new soul.

Contributors

▼▼▼▼▼▼▼▼▼▼▼▼▼▼▼▼▼▼▼▼▼▼▼▼▼▼▼▼▼▼▼▼▼▼▼

Chinua Achebe was born at Ogidi in Eastern Nigeria, educated at Government College, Umuahia, and the University of Ibadan. Between 1954 and 1966 he worked for the Nigerian Broadcasting Corporation. He has published four novels – *Things Fall Apart* (1958), *No Longer at Ease* (1960), *Arrow of God* (1964) and *A Man of the People* (1966). He has also published his stories under the title *Girls at War* and his poems in a book called *Beware, Soul Brother*. He was the founding editor of the African Writers Series.

Ama Ata Aidoo was born and educated in Ghana, received her first degree at the University of Ghana and attended an advanced course in Creative Writing at Stanford University in California. She has written two plays which have been published – *Dilemma of a Ghost* (1965) and *Anowa* (1970) – and a collection of short stories, *No Sweetness Here*. Her poems have been published in various places.

J. P. Clark, Nigerian poet, playwright and critic, was born in 1935 in the Ijaw area of the Niger Delta, and educated at the University College of Ibadan (where he founded the poetry magazine, *The Horn*). He has worked as a journalist and went as a Parvin fellow at Princeton University in the United States. He has published and had produced four plays – *Song of a Goat*, *Masquerade*, *The Raft* and *Ozidi* – and his poetry has been published by both Mbari, Ibadan and Longmans.

Birago Diop was born in 1906, French West African short-story writer and poet. Born at Dakar into a middle-class Wolof family from Senegal. He had a brilliant school career, then qualified as a veterinary surgeon at the Toulouse Veterinary School. In 1945 he became head of the Zoo-Technical services of the Haute-Volta. After Senegal became independent (1960), he was appointed Senegalese ambassador in Tunis.

Birago Diop showed early literary aptitude, and wrote poems inspired by the esoteric African circumcision rites. But it was not until 1960 that he published his first book of verse, *Leurres et lueurs*, a sort of anthology of his experiences. His real fame rests on his short stories, *Contes d'Amadou Koumba* (Paris, 1947; also tr. into Russian), and *Nouveaux contes d'Amadou Koumba* (Paris, 1958) with a preface by L. S. Senghor. While posing modestly as a mere interpreter of the naïve tales of his village *griot* or storyteller, he cleverly evokes the poetic inspiration of his native land.

Nadine Gordimer was born and lives in South Africa. She is the author of five novels and five short story collections. She received the W. H. Smith Award in 1961. She lives in Johannesburg.

Cheikh Hamidou Kane is Senegalese and was born in 1928. His novel is available in an English translation under the title *Ambiguous Adventure* and it has been described as 'the most characteristic statement in imaginative terms of the fundamental outlook of French African Writers'.

Joseph Kariuki was born in Kenya in 1929, attended Makerere College in Uganda and, after several years teaching in Kenya, read English at King's College, Cambridge. He returned to Kenya in 1962 and became Principal of the Institute of Public Administration. He then went to Addis Ababa and Tangier to work for United Nations' agencies.

Camara Laye was born in Guinea in 1928. *The African Child*, *The Radiance of the King* and *A Dream of Africa* all appear in English translations, but he has also written other books.

Ali A. Mazrui is Professor and Head of the Department of Political Science and Public Administration at Makerere. He was born in Mombasa, Kenya, in 1933 and studied at Manchester, Columbia and Oxford. He is an associate editor of *Transition* and co-editor of *Mawazo*. He has published a number of books including: *Towards a Pax Africana*; *The Anglo-African Commonwealth*; *On Heroes and Uhuru-Worship*; *Violence and Thought*; and *Protest and Power in Black Africa* (co-editor), and also a novel, *The Trial of Christopher Okigbo*.

S. Okechukwu Mezu, a Nigerian, is an Associate Professor at the State University of New York, Buffalo. He is the author of the novel *Behind the Rising Sun* and two books on Senghor, one in English and one in French. He is the editor of several other books and runs *The Black Academy Press*.

Lewis Nkosi was born in South Africa in 1936. He is a broadcaster, journalist, essayist and playwright and now lives in London. He worked for *Drum* and *Post* in Johannesburg for many years. He has published a play *The Rhythm of Violence* and *Home and Exile* a book of essays and articles. He was literary editor of the *The New African*.

Okello Oculi was born in Lang'o, northern Uganda, in 1942 and educated at Soroti College, St Peter's College (Tororo) and at St Mary's College (Kisubi) before completing his B.A. in political science at Makerere

University, Uganda. During his undergraduate days he was News Editor of *The Makererean* and, as an exchange student, spent a year at Stanford University in California. His book-length poem, *Orphan*, was published by East African Publishing House in 1968, followed in the same year by *Prostitute*, a novel he wrote while continuing his studies at Essex University in England. A columnist for the Uganda newspaper, *The People*, Oculi is currently at Makerere working on a doctoral thesis in political science.

Gabriel Okara was born in 1921 in the Ijaw District of the Niger Delta. He trained as book-binder but has worked in the Information Services of Eastern Nigeria. He has published short stories, film scripts and one novel, *The Voice*, and his poems have been published in England, America, Sweden, West Germany, and Italy as well as throughout Africa.

Sembène Ousmane was born in 1923 in Senegal. He is the author of several books of which the following are available in English translations: *God's Bits of Wood*, *The Money-Order*, *White Genesis* and *Voltaique*.

David Rubadiri was born in Malawi in 1930, educated at King's College, Budo and at Makerere College, Kampala. In 1964 he became Malawi's first ambassador to the United States and the United Nations and is currently lecturing at Makerere College.

Ousmane Socé is Senegalese and has published five books of which the best-known is the novel *Karim*.

Tchicaya U Tam'si was born in Congo Brazzaville in 1931. His large corpus of poetry is represented in English by a book of translations by Gerald Moore called *Selected Poems*.

Index

▼▼▼▼▼▼▼▼▼▼▼▼▼▼▼▼▼▼▼▼▼▼▼▼▼▼▼▼▼▼▼▼▼